MORE LETTERS AND POEMS OF

THE
KEATS
CIRCLE

MORE LETTERS AND POEMS OF

THE

KEATS

CIRCLE

HYDER EDWARD ROLLINS

HARVARD UNIVERSITY PRESS
CAMBRIDGE · MASSACHUSETTS
1955

CONTENTS

			Page
INTRODUCTION			1
LETTERS AND POEMS			11

No.	Date	Writer	Recipient	
1	1814	George Keats	Fanny Keats	11
2	January 30, 1820	George Keats	Fanny Keats	12
3	January 7, 1822	George Keats	Fanny Keats	14
4	February, 1824	George Keats	Fanny Keats	16
5	April 28, May (?), 1824	George Keats	Fanny Keats	19
6	February, 1825	George Keats	Fanny Keats	23
7	March 18, 1825	George Keats	Richard Abbey	27
8	June 5, 1825	George Keats	Fanny Keats	29
9	March 4, April 15, 1826	George Keats	Fanny Llanos	31
10	April 9, 1826	L. Manning	Fanny Llanos	36
11	May 23, 1827	George Keats	Fanny Llanos	37
12	March 25, 1828	George Keats	Fanny Llanos	40
13	June (?), 1828	George Keats	Fanny Llanos	41
14	July 10, 11, 1828	George Keats	Valentin Llanos	44
15	July 12, 1828	George Keats	Fanny Llanos	47
16	March 5, 1829	George Keats	Fanny Llanos	51
17	November 15, 1829	George Keats	The Llanoses	53
18	November 22, 1830	George Keats	Fanny Llanos	57
19	January 3, 1831 (?)	Valentin Llanos	George Keats	58
20	March 24, 1831	George Keats	The Llanoses	63

			Page
No.	*Date*	*Writer*	*Recipient*	

No.	*Date*	*Writer*	*Recipient*	*Page*
21	May 6, 1832	George Keats	John Hamilton Reynolds	65
22	May 6 (?), 1832	George Keats	Fanny Llanos	67
23	May (?), 1832	Fanny Llanos (?)	George Keats	70
24	Undated	George Keats: Two Poems		72
25	July 3, 1861	Joseph Severn	Fanny Llanos	74
26	September 21, 1861	Joseph Severn	Fanny Llanos	75
27	September 21, 1861	Joseph Severn	Fanny Llanos	76
28	November 5, 1861	Joseph Severn	Fanny Llanos	78
29	August 22, 1862	Joseph Severn	Fanny Llanos	80
30	February, March, 1867	Joseph Severn	Fanny Llanos	82
31	March 29, 1869	Joseph Severn	Fanny Llanos	86
32	December 8, 1870	Joseph Severn	Fanny Llanos	88
33	February 24, 1871	Joseph Severn	Fanny Llanos	91
34	May 9, 1872	Joseph Severn	Fanny Llanos	93
35	May 28, 1873	Joseph Severn	Fanny Llanos	95
36	July 15, 1873	Joseph Severn	Fanny Llanos	97
37	August 5, 1877	Joseph Severn	Fanny Llanos	99
38	February 12, 1878	Sir Charles W. Dilke	Fanny Llanos	101
39	April 7, 1878	Emma Frances Keats Speed	Fanny Llanos	103
40	May 25, 1879	Emma Frances Keats Speed	Fanny Llanos	105
	APPENDIX			107
41	February 6, 1821	John Taylor	Joseph Severn	109
42	February 12, 1821	J. A. Hessey	Joseph Severn	112
43	February 27, 1821	J. A. Hessey	Joseph Severn	116
	INDEX OF NAMES AND TITLES			119

MORE LETTERS AND POEMS OF

THE
KEATS
CIRCLE

INTRODUCTION

I

In 1953 Dr. Ernesto Paradinas y Brockmann,[1] of Avila, Spain, sold a number of letters and notes written by or to his great-grandmother, Fanny Keats de Llanos, sister of John Keats, to Mr. Arthur A. Houghton, Jr., who then generously gave them to the Harvard Keats Collection. Among them are a few oddly stilted and unrevealing letters from Señora Llanos to various members of her family and many more from Joseph Severn, H. Buxton Forman, Sir Charles W. Dilke, and the American children and grandchildren of George Keats.

By far the most interesting and important items are the forty connected with George Keats, Fanny Keats, and Severn herewith printed. In the first group (1814–1832) there are twenty letters written by George Keats: fifteen to Fanny Keats, one to her Spanish husband Valentin Llanos y Gutierrez, two jointly to Fanny and Llanos, and one each to Richard Abbey, long the guardian of the Keats children, and to John Hamilton Reynolds, perhaps John Keats's closest friend. The other items are one letter each from Valentin and Fanny Llanos to George Keats, one from Miss L. Manning, a previously unheard of friend, to Fanny, and two autograph poems by George which show that the poetic mantle of John did not fall on his brother's shoulders. The second group (1861–1879) contains sixteen letters to Señora Llanos, thirteen by Severn, one by Sir Charles W. Dilke, and two by George's daughter, Emma Frances Speed. One of George's letters was printed in 1883 by Forman, who also gave very brief extracts from four others. But, on the whole, this new collection, small as it is, presents fresh information that

---

[1] See Willard B. Pope's account (with a picture of the doctor, his wife, and his eight children) of a visit to him in the *Keats-Shelley Journal,* II (1953), 118.

will necessitate a partial rewriting of the biographies of the personages concerned.

It is a pity that these documents turned up too late to be included, where they really belong, in *The Keats Circle* (1948), for most of them answer or are answered by letters in those volumes or explain matters therein discussed. Like *The Keats Circle* itself, they give many facts of interest about the poet but far more about his relatives and his acquaintances, the Brawnes, Reynolds, James Rice, Abbey, C. W. Dilke, Joseph Severn, as well as incidental information about Taylor and Hessey, Michael Drury, Wilkinson, and others whose names are familiar to every student of the poet.

George Keats no doubt was, as he claims (No. 6), the person who best understood his brother, the only one "who was fitted to releive him of its [the world's] friction." Almost every word he wrote is, in one way or another, a vital part of the poet's biography, and probably scholars will never cease arguing whether he did or did not treat his brother unfairly in financial matters. The question of George's probity, fought over so bitterly by Charles Brown and William Haslam versus Dilke in the 1820's, turns up in every contemporary life of the poet.

These new letters throw brilliant light on the actions and characters of George Keats and Fanny Keats and her husband. The earliest letter by any member of the Keats family yet found, No. 1 below, was written by George to Fanny in 1814. But he was not a punctilious correspondent, and after he had left England in 1820, for the second time, without telling Fanny goodbye (No. 2), they were more or less estranged. For a short while John Keats kept Fanny informed of George's doings, but during his long, final illness in England and Italy, and after his death, they drifted literally a whole world apart.

The fault lay chiefly with Fanny, who had heard, perhaps from the Reynoldses or Haslam (she did not know Brown), of George's alleged heartlessness and dishonesty in stripping his brother of money to carry back to Kentucky. She and John had been devoted, and the letters he wrote to her are perfect examples of how an older person should address a child. On the contrary, George and Fanny were not really sympathetic. With a wife and children, he found it hard to grasp and sympathize with her girlish problems, and he could never cast off a sort of elder brother's patronizing and stuffiness. Though John Keats's fiancée, Fanny Brawne, had defended George in a letter of May, 1821,[2] Fanny Keats, unconvinced, remained silent, while from Louisville the puzzled George wrote several letters of complaint. Even the letter (see No. 3) in which he "commiserated" with her on John's death was unacknowledged. In February, 1824 (No. 4), he lamented, "The last time I heard from you was thro' our dear John." Fanny did write at least once before May, 1824 (see No. 5), but she had large reservations about his dishonorable conduct until the following August, when Mrs. Dilke persuaded her that he "is still and ever will be an honourable man." [3]

None the less, Fanny never confided in George, even when she was in love with and then engaged to Llanos. Instead she merely wrote cryptically (see No. 5) about her supposed Spanish-looking face and about a "change of life" she was contemplating, the latter remark being interpreted by George as meaning that she was ill-advised enough to contemplate moving from the home of her guardian Abbey. Automatically he expostulated, urging her to remain with that "straightforward, candid man." Fanny had always disliked both Abbey and his wife, and the chief irritant she found in George's letters was his unfailing praise of that "good man Mʳ Abbey." Then, as she came of age, she feared that Abbey, after a series of business reverses, had jeopardized her inheritance. Fanny Brawne (June 16, 1824), to be sure, attempted to remove these fears. "My brother," she wrote, thinks there is "not the slightest reason to alarm yourself as Mʳ A. is considered beyond all dispute as a man of large property—The *losses* you mentioned are well known in the city

---

[2] *Letters of F.B.*, pp. 33f.　　　　　　　　[3] Adami, p. 108.

but he is considered very rich in spite of them." [4] But Fanny Keats's apprehensions were irremovable, and it could hardly have been pleasing when George in February, 1824 (No. 4), harped as usual on Abbey in "whose integrity, and goodness of Heart the utmost reliance may be placed." John had known of his sister's unhappiness as a ward of the Abbeys, and had tactfully advised her how to deal with them. On the contrary, George, in addition to praising Abbey's goodness, urged her (No. 5) not to "intrust any one but Mr Abbey with your property" just when Fanny, more fearful than ever that he had squandered or stolen all her money, had left Abbey's house. Undoubtedly she took the keenest satisfaction in writing to George on May 31, 1826, about the machinations of "that consummate villain Abbey"—and in announcing casually her marriage. "We are doing every thing in our power," she went on, "to oblige Abbey to refund the money; but I fear we shall not be successful. I thought you knew he was not an honest man from principle, but merely because he had no occasion to rob being at the time you were in England possessed of considerable property." [5] George's surprise and disillusionment (No. 9) are almost comical, yet he took Fanny to task for not having earlier disclosed the villainy, and characteristically added that she had endangered his own prospects by failing to do so.

The usual story has been, as Edgcumbe phrases it, that "Fanny Keats had considerable difficulty in obtaining from Richard Abbey the money of which he had control. Charles Wentworth Dilke came to her aid, and eventually she received not only her share of the money left by her grandmother, but also that due to her from the estates of her brothers John and Tom." [6] Mrs. Adami agrees that "Dilke came to her help and dealt with Abbey firmly enough to obtain all that belonged to her." [7] Actually

---

[4] *Letters of F.B.*, p. 97.
[5] *KC* I, 297f.
[6] *Letters of F.B.*, p. 99.
[7] Adami, p. 117.

Valentin Llanos (No. 19) claimed the credit for forcing Abbey to mortgage and then sell his Walthamstow property to repay Fanny Llanos, and both the Llanoses severely criticize Dilke for his inactive, almost hostile, role. The letters (No. 19–23) discussing Abbey's financial shenanigans and giving particulars about the troubles of the Llanoses and George with the unbusinesslike law firm of Rice and Reynolds, John Keats's dear friends, and its successor, Reynolds and Simmons (or Symons), show clearly that a full and complete account of the settling of the Keats estate is yet to be written.

George's illusions about Abbey, then Fanny's concern with her immediate family, imperiled their attachment, and at times both wrote brusquely. As a good businessman, George was disturbed by Llanos' disastrous or impractical schemes for making money by selling newfangled bridle bits in England or by exporting wine to America, and he said so with considerable vigor. As his own wealth accumulated, however, he generously instructed his and Fanny's shaky (he feared shady) London lawyers to see that she got all the money due her from Abbey before his own claim was considered, although, again as a man of business, he expressed great eagerness for every penny owing to him.

The correspondence is a melancholy record of misunderstandings. Fanny Llanos, indeed, nursed an imaginary grievance about George's supposed neglect of her, his indifference to her welfare. She took him harshly to task for not having transported her from London to Louisville, complaining that his rare invitations had been formal and insincere. George defended himself (No. 22) bluntly but with good humor, only to have Llanos write for her to copy a note (No. 23) phrased in the coldest, most unsisterly language, reproaching George for his failure to make a loan of £100 she had requested. It is remarkable, too, that when Mrs. George Keats and her children visited London in 1828–1829 the Llanoses paid almost no attention to them (No. 16). That the relations between brother and sister continued to be strained and then became nonexistent was in the main the latter's fault. After the Llanoses moved to Spain in the summer of 1833, George had no word from them at least up to March, 1838.[8] Perhaps he had none before he died on December 24, 1841, and certainly Fanny knew nothing of his death until late in 1848.[9] No doubt regretting the past, henceforth, as the Paradinas collection proves, she kept on fairly close terms by correspondence with George's family, no member of which she ever actually saw.

Few as the letters are, they tell many other interesting things about the tangled finances of the Keats children: as when George (to his honor) instructs Abbey to pay debts contracted by his brother to the amount of £319, and observes that the latter had loaned to the lawyer Wilkinson £50 which had not been repaid; or when the Llanoses, who owed George some £616, plaintively rehearse their almost hopeless dealings with Abbey, Rice, Reynolds, and Dilke. They also give previously unknown facts about Fanny Llanos' various London addresses, her friendship with Miss Manning, the date of her departure for Spain, her staunch defense of Fanny Brawne that forced George, who had long regarded Miss Brawne as "an artful bad hearted Girl," to change his opinion. George himself in a remarkably detached, if engaging, fashion analyzes the characters of his wife and children; gives the dates, not before recorded, of the death of his daughter Rosalind and the birth of Isabel; tells anecdotes about some personal friends like Charles Briggs and John Bull; and establishes pretty closely the dates of his wife's departure for Europe and her return to New York. He emerges from the correspondence as an intelligent, cool-headed, attractive gentleman who was entirely worthy of the respect and deference paid to him by his great brother.

---

[8] *KC* II, 32.
[9] *KC* II, 251.

II

When the letters of George Keats ended in 1832, Fanny Llanos was a happy, somewhat self-centered young matron. In March, 1861, when she, her husband, and her children Juan and Rosa joined her son-in-law and daughter, Leopold and Isabel Llanos Brockmann, in Rome, she was a serene grandmother of fifty-eight. The preceding January, Joseph Severn, after a twenty-years' residence in England, had been appointed British consul at Rome, where he was, as he continued to be, widely known and admired. "His geniality," said the painter George Richmond, "charmed every member of the Roman society, from high officials at the Vatican to the humblest traveller," and in his house "were to be found the foremost men and women of the day." [10]

Appropriately enough, Fanny Llanos first met Severn by accident on April 6 in the very room where her brother John had died. The meeting was a shock but a delight to both. "For a long time," Severn wrote, "we remained without being able to speak. 'Twas like a brother and sister who had parted in early life meeting after forty years." [11] Severn immediately took the whole Llanos-Brockmann family into his heart, and although his personal association with them was brief (they left Italy in the fall of 1864), the friendship, kept alive by correspondence, was terminated only by his death in 1879. His thirteen letters that Fanny Llanos preserved (various others failed to reach her) were written at intervals between 1861 and 1877, when Severn's age was from sixty-seven to eighty-three. In their shaky spelling and unsteady handwriting, no less than in their forgetful repetitiousness, they show the deteriorating effects of age, but they also show how to the end of his long life he venerated, indeed worshiped, the memory of "the illustrious poet" whose unextinguished spirit had already successfully pleaded against

[10] Anna M. W. Stirling, *The Richmond Papers* (London, 1926), p. 43.
[11] Adami, p. 155.

Oblivion for the name "Severn." The painter William Bewick
had written of him in November, 1850: "His tenderness and
affection for the poet was as strong as the love of a woman; and
as I knew Keats, poor fellow, I now love my friend Severn. . .
He is as honourable and dear a fellow as ever breathed, with a
noble and generous spirit, and the feeling of a true gentleman." [12]

The thirteen letters fill small gaps in Mrs. Adami's biography
of Fanny Keats, making it evident, for instance, that the
Llanoses and the Brockmanns left Rome early in July, 1861,
for Naples, where they remained for over a year. They also give
previously unrecorded facts about Fanny's residences, her
friends (Emma Novello, Lord Ampthill, the Countess of Castle
Stewart, and others), and various members of her family—her
son Luis, who seems in 1873 to have been connected with the
Spanish embassy in Rome, Count Brockmann, her son-in-law,
who invented some sort of an impractical contraption "for the
bridge twixt Dover & Calais," and Rosa, her musical daughter,
as "the *pearl*," or most beautiful figure, in Severn's picture,
"The Marriage of Cana."

About himself Severn is only incidentally informative, but
whenever a first-rate biography is written these letters will have
to be taken into account. His biographers, William Sharp and
the Countess of Birkenhead, no doubt would have been interested in his comments on the slow progress of "The Marriage
of Cana," "the best of all my works," on the date at which he
moved into the Palazzo Poli, and on the structural changes
made in that house during later years. Very interesting are his
observations about the attacks on himself as consul by six
Englishmen, "even to killing me of[f]," his relations with the
king of Italy, and his apparently unwise investment of £1000 in
stock of the new Marcian Acqueduct. Of considerable interest,
too, are the remarks about his two pensions, the one hundred
thirty prisoners of the Vatican whose liberation he had secured,

[12] Thomas Landseer, *Life and Letters of William Bewick* (London, 1871),
II, 150.

the "imprisonment" of the pope in 1871, and the enormous changes brought into the life of Rome when it displaced Florence as the capital. His offhand references to ill health are melancholy reminders that old age itself is a disease, but those to his children are always proudly cheerful.

Severn's wife died before she could join him at the consulate, and, after his sons and daughters married, he was a very lonely man. Naturally he was pleased by the fine marriages they all, in spite of being a poor artist's children, had made. Especially gratifying was Arthur's marriage to the beautiful Joan Agnew, ward and cousin of "the great Art Critic" John Ruskin, who at least pretended to rank Arthur as a painter with his adored Joseph Turner. But when the even more talented Ann Mary Severn Newton, who had painted various members of the royal family, died in 1866, Severn sustained a blow from which, he told the sympathetic Señora Llanos, he never expected to recover. With the unconscious pathos of the aged, in three different letters he reminded her of how "odd" it felt to have no responsibilities but himself: "I have always been thinking of others & *never of myself.*" But the lack of responsibilities merely increased his loneliness, and as old age steadily crept on he became more and more sentimental about Keats and Fanny. Letters to or from her inevitably brought vivid recollections of the bitter, if painfully dear, period, the finest in his life, when from September, 1820, to February, 1821, he had tenderly watched over the dying poet and thereby gained a kind of immortality. Small wonder that he missed the "charming" Llanos family, always hoped that they would revisit Rome, and described in 1869 his meeting with Fanny as "a romance *aye & is so still.*" To her he wrote his final letter on August 5, 1877, fifty-seven years after he had escorted her brother to Rome, in it telling of "a life size portrait of the illustrious Poet" he was beginning and of "a picture of Isabella & the pot of Basil I have just done." Severn died on August 3, 1879. He was a good man—a far better man than artist—whose name should always be mentioned with honor. If his letters are without literary value and are, indeed, rather pitiful, that is primarily the fault of Time, the devourer of everything, even goodness.

In the final letters of the present series, Sir Charles W. Dilke, grandson of Keats's friend, informed Mme. Llanos of Harry Buxton Forman's having published Keats's love letters to Fanny Brawne (1878), an editorial act of which he vigorously and vehemently disapproved, and added a remarkable statement about the incompleteness of that book; while George Keats's daughter, Emma Frances Speed, comments on the love letters and on the poet's tombstone, which she had helped restore.

Fanny Llanos died at Madrid on December 16, 1889, nearly sixty-nine years after her brother John's death in Rome. She had outlived George Keats by forty-eight and her admirer Severn by ten years. She was in no sense a rival of Dorothy Wordsworth, but because of her associations she has, like George Keats, a definite place in English literary history.

III

The three letters recently acquired by the Harvard Keats Collection and added in the Appendix present Keats's publishers in a strange, new light—and add to one's sympathy for Severn's trials. If it be thought that they have an excess of "evangelicalism," at any rate they show how dearly Taylor and Hessey loved their young poet-friend, and how highly and truly they valued Severn's services to him.[13]

[13] The following works are cited only by the name of their authors: Marie Adami, *Fanny Keats* (London, 1937) ; the Countess of Birkenhead, *Against Oblivion: The Life of Joseph Severn* (London, 1943); William Sharp, *The Life and Letters of Joseph Severn* (London, 1892). *The Keats Circle*, ed. Hyder E. Rollins (2 vols.; Harvard University Press, 1948), is cited as *KC*; M. B. Forman's *The Letters of John Keats* (Oxford University Press, 1952) as *Letters*; Fred Edgcumbe's *Letters of Fanny Brawne to Fanny Keats* (Oxford University Press, 1936) as *Letters of F.B.*; H. B. Forman's *The Poetical Works and Other Writings of John Keats* (4 vols.; London, 1883) as *F*.

Canceled letters or words in the documents are printed in shaped brackets (⟨⟩), letters or words torn off or erased in curly braces ({}), editorial insertions in square brackets ([]). Three asterisks (***) indicate that part of the letter is missing.

GEORGE KEATS TO FANNY KEATS
1 8 1 4 [1]

Address: To/ Miss. F. M. Keats

Pancras Lane

My dearest Fanny

I herewith send you a peice of silk and pastboard to make
⟨me⟩ a shade for my Eyes, which you will have the goodness
when finished to return to M^r [2] Abbey's who I have no doubt
will be so good as to forward it to Pancras Lane. With this you
will receive a skipping-rope which I purchased in order to
encourage you to jump and skipp about, to avoid those nasty
Chilblanes that so troubled you last Winter, perhaps Mr Bourke
will teach you the skipping-rope hornpipe, you can as well prac-
tice it in play hours by way of Amusement, and at the same time
improvement. Your poor Grandmother has been very ill indeed, but she is now recovering fast, she desires her love to you.
Your brothers join in their love to you, and hope you use all
your endeavours to improve, particularly in music; I can assure
you they love you most affectionately, and will do any thing in
their power to make you happy which I have no doubt will
succeed provided you will at the same time make yourself *good.*
I am now happy in subscribing myself the first Time
Dearest Sister
Your most affectionate Brother
George Keats
Let me have the shade as soon as possible—in the note I say that
your Brothers love you—mind—I mean to include myself—
Friday morning—

[1] Fanny Keats was visiting someone, probably her guardian Richard Abbey
at Walthamstow, during the illness of her grandmother, Alice (Mrs. John)
Jennings, who died shortly before December 14, 1814. George wrote, on paper
watermarked with the date 1814, from his quarters above Abbey's counting

room at 4 Pancras Lane, Cheapside. He calls the letter his first to his sister, and it is the earliest yet found by any of the Keats family.

² *Originally* M^{rs}.

->>> 2 <<<-

GEORGE KEATS TO FANNY KEATS[1]

3 0 January 1 8 2 0

Printed by *F*, IV, 391–393.[2]

Liverpool—Sunday Morn—Jany. 30th 1819[3]—

My dear Fanny

I considered not taking a final leave of you a misfortune, and regretted very much that constant occupation detained me from coming to Walthamstow; but now I look upon the pain attending the last good bye, and shake of the hand as well spared, and reflect on the pleasure of seeing you again at however remote a period; when you will be a *Woman* and I a '*bald Pate.*' I arrived here last night after a rather disagreeable ride of 36 hours, and engaged a passage in the Courier—Captn Eldridge, for New York before I went to bed; she will sail on the first, Tuesday next. In this said English Feather bed I was in a greater risk to lose my life than thro' all my journey from Louisville to London. Before going to bed I thought it prudent to clear my stomach of bile, and took calomel; a cold taken while this is operating on the system frequently proves fatal, it opens the pores of the skin, and allows the inflamation to lay complete hold of one. Not having slept for two nights, I remained dead asleep while water was dripping thro' the ceiling untill it had penetrated through [4] all the clothes, the feather bed and the mattrass. The instant I awoke I jumped out of bed, called the Servants and was put into a fresh bed, fully expecting to be laid up, but this morning to my astonishment I find myself well; you see if I can stand water when it nearly floats me in my bed without injury, I cannot be born to be drowned. Mr Abbey behaved very kindly to me before I left for which I am sure you will feel grateful. He is attentive in his commerce with his fellows in all essentials. He observes with pleasure, the pleasure communicated to others; he says you sometimes look thin and pale, but he thinks that you have been better since you have run about a little feeding chickens, attending your little Cat &c. A man of coarse feeling would never notice these things. He expressed surprise that neither you nor Miss A.—⟨should not speak⟩ spoke at meals; so you see it is not his wish that you should be moped and silent, therefore cheer up and look lively as nature made you.[5] I shall hear from John from time to time about you, as you will of me. I am

dear Fanny

Your very affectionate Brother

George.

[1] In pencil on the upper left-hand corner Fred Holland Day, during a visit to the Llanos family at Madrid (see Rollins and Parrish, *Keats and the Bostonians* [Harvard University Press, 1951], pp. 5–7), wrote, "Copied/ FD./ Dec. '90."

[2] On June 18, 1881, H. B. Forman wrote to Fanny Keats de Llanos, returning the three letters of her brother George which she had lent to him. He also made some use of two others in the 1883 edition of Keats.

[3] *F* 1820. Actually George left London in the early morning of January 28, 1820 (*Letters,* p. 455). He also misdated the letter, very similar to this one, that he wrote to John Keats on January 30 (*Letters,* p. 456).

[4] *F* thro'.

[5] Keats refers to this matter in his letter of February 6, 1820, to Fanny (*Letters,* p. 458).

123573

→≫ 3 ≪←

GEORGE KEATS TO FANNY KEATS

7 January 1 8 2 2

Address: per favour of Mr C. Wylie./ Miss F. M. Keats/ 4 Pancrass Lane/ London/ At. Richard Abbey Esq^{r's}/ One brief extract—"I had hoped before . . . make you comfortable"—is printed by *F*, IV, 395f.

Louisville. Kentucky. Jan 7. 1822

My dearest Fanny

I have to entreat your forgiveness for not writing more frequently, but what can I write about; my affairs do not go on so badly or prosperously as to be worth communicating, of the manners of the People and of the country in which we live you were fully informed in my former letters. Its politics varying every day would be interesting only to the lovers and haters of democracy; to you such discussions would be dulness. To be sure our health might be communicated from time to time, but when we feel ourselves well it seems thinking much of ourselves to put you to the expense of letters to inform you of it, when we are sick we delay writing untill we can send better news. Nothing to say, seems a common foolish excuse, altho I must urge it; at this distance with posts so uncertain and dilatory, we cannot indulge ourselves with the form of a regular correspondence, the space of 6 months between question and answer is enough to freeze the most interesting subject; All we can hope for is that nature and education have formed our hearts to retain affection without the assistance of adventitious circumstances. I hope four or five years will bring us to England, to effect this grand object I work early and late, with industry and perseverance that astonishes the lazy Kentuckians, this coming year I expect to reap my harvest; last year I should have done *very well* but for the extreme sickliness of the season; besides being ⟨ailing⟩ positively confined to my bed 3 mos as well as my

dear Wife and younges[t] child Rosaline,[1] we were ailing 2
mos more, the child is still poorly. Extra of my *former* expenses and the loss attending the Mill's not working 3 mos
(in consequence of the sickness of the hands, and mine) I spent
£150. This has been a heavy trial to us, but thank God, we met
the last day in the year in the same circumstances and spirits
that we began it. I hoped before this to receive [2] from you an
answer of my letter to you, commiserating with you on the death
of our dear Brother; that dreadful misfortune leaves us more
necessary to each others happiness; it leaves me your natural
Guardian and if circumstances should throw you from under
the Protection of that good Man Mr Abbey, I have a happy and
cheerful home to make you comfortable. The Gentleman (M^r
Brooks,[3] stationer, Oxford Street.) who will bring this, will
probably return to America, I will direct him to advise you
when, and shall expect ⟨the⟩ your memoirs by him, however you
must write directly by post, as much as can be put in a sheet of
letter paper. Your Sister and prattling neice [4] desire their love,
but that M^r A's family live so retired I should request Mrs Keats'
Brother's and Mother [5] to come and see you and invite you out,
but I am persuaded such a proceeding would displease them,
and we owe them too much to treat their wishes with disrespect.
I shall enclose this to Charles Wylie and direct him to deliver it
personally, if Mrs A. pleases to invite him to repeat his call all
will be well, if not he is too proud to go where he is not welcome.[6] He has been educated a merchant, and is as far as I can
learn clever, I am sure he has a good heart. Present my respects
to M^r M^rs and Miss Abbey. I will write to M^r A by this opportunity   I fear he thinks I am doing badly, it is true I have not
done well, but I have stemmed the torrent of bad success,
obtained some experience, and am now sailing steadily towards
success.

 I am, my dear Fanny, Your affectionate Friend & Brother

       George Keats.

[1] Or Rosalind (died 1826). See pp. 34f., below.

[2] *F* to have received.

[3] John Brooks, 421 Oxford Street. See *KC* I, 170.

[4] Georgiana Emily (1819–1856), later Mrs. Alfred Gwathmey.

[5] Charles and Henry Wylie and Mrs. James Wylie.

[6] Fanny Brawne wrote to Fanny Keats in August, 1822 (*Letters of F.B.*, p. 75): "I met M*r* Wylie a short time ago, and he told me he believed his brother had called on you."

->» 4 «<-

GEORGE KEATS TO FANNY KEATS

February 1824

Address: Miss. F. Keats./–to the care of Rich*d* Abbey Esq*re*/ Pancrass Lane/ London/ England

My dear Fanny   Louisville. Kentucky. North America

The time is so long since I heard of or from you, that I must again endeavour to obtain some intelligence thro' the medium of the post, altho' it has so often failed. I cannot suppose for an instant that you have neglected to answer the letters you have rec*d* if indeed they have come to hand; either your's or mine have invariably miscarried, and continual disappointment makes me despair of hearing from you more: I shall however try every means before I give up with the feeling that you no longer desire the correspondence. The last time I heard from you was thro' our dear John,[1] whose loss if possible renders us more interesting to each other and leaves me your only natural protector. While you are under the care of M*r* Abbey I feel comparatively easy knowing him to be a man upon whose integrity, and goodness of Heart the utmost reliance may be placed.[2] In the mean time it is well that we should understand from each other our mutual progress in life, in the hope that our fates assisted by our inclinations will eventually bring us together, I should be most unhappy to give up the Idea of again seeing you and the glorious land that gave me birth. M*rs* Keats is continually speaking of you, and never having had a sister herself builds much on an intimate connection with you, and I am persuaded that had you the slightest knowledge of her character you would look with the greatest pleasure to the time when you will become acquainted with her. It must be somewhat interesting to you to have two little neices who, in learning their Alphabet say F for Fanny, and talk about aunt Fanny.—The eldest is a very clever child and can read a little, has very dark eyes something like John in the face, and is called most beautiful, her name is Georgiana, the second Rosalind has dark eyes but of a light complection and hair like your's used to be, she is called very pretty but is not so quick as Georgiana perhaps in consequence of having suffered so much sickness, she is now in good health, our youngest Emma Frances is the beauty of the place and the best child we have had, she has however suffered much from sickness and somewhat backward in consequence. With so many young children we of course live a very domestic life and I believe as comfortable a one as any Family within my experience. Our circumstances will not allow us to associate with what is called the first or in other words the richest people here, yet whenever we come in contact with them in public places we are treated with the utmost respect. Ever since I have been in this country business has become worse and worse, and money more and more scarce, it is as much [as] I can do with the most persevering attention to business to obtain more *money* than sufficient to pay my expences; I am now living in a House that exactly suits me, situated most pleasantly on a high Bank looking on to the Falls of the Ohio, it was built by the concern in which I am the acting partner and one third owner for my residence, being immediately in the neighbourhood of our steam Saw Mill. If I had the same talent for drawing that I had when you were a child I would sketch it for you. Last year was the first year that I realized more than my expenses, and my prospects next year are I think better, but my sanguine temperament has so often misled me, that I do not depend so much on good prospects as heretofore, should I ever be in positive distress you shall hear, should I become rich you shall see me in England. I hope my dear Sister that you will ans{wer} this immediately giving me an exact account of your state {of} mind, your occupation, progress in music and reading, what books you like, where you cheifly spend your time and with whom, be assured my dear Fanny that whatever you write will be interesting, and that when I become acquainted with what would be amusing to you, my letters will be more amusing and longer. Mrs Keats and the Children send their love. Make my best respects to M^rs M^r and Miss Abbey and tell M^r A that I have been hard pushed to make "the ends of the year meet" but that last year my circumstances were bettered, and that my prospects are good.—M^rs K has enjoyed good health but I have suffered much in purse as well as pain by sickness.—

I am

My dear Fanny

Your very Affectionate Brother George

February 1824

¹ The last known letter of John Keats to George was written on November 12, 1819 (*Letters,* pp. 440–443, where it is misdated November 19), but the latter visited England in January, 1820. George here refers to some lost letter. Fanny Keats had not written because (like Charles Brown and William Haslam) she believed that George had taken advantage of John in money matters. Though Fanny Brawne (*Letters of F.B.,* pp. 33f.) had defended him as early as May 23, 1821, and though Fanny Keats did write before May, 1824 (see the next letter), it was only in August, 1824, that Mrs. Dilke (see Adami, p. 108) convinced his sister "that George is still and ever will be an honourable man." "I sincerely hate myself," Fanny added, "for having for an instant doubted it." None the less, as the following letters show, she and George continued to have misunderstandings and doubts.

² George's faith in Abbey lasted for two further years. See his letter of March 4, 1826, below.

≫≫ 5 ≪≪

GEORGE KEATS TO FANNY KEATS
2 8 April, May (?) 1 8 2 4

Address: Miss Keats./ Care of Richd Abbey Esqre/ Pancrass Lane/ London
Brief extracts are printed by *F*, IV, 399–401.

Louisville, Kentucky, April 28th 1824

My dear Fanny.

> 'Tis now the early budders are just new
> And spread in mazes of the youngest hue
> About old Forests" [1]

This season never comes round without reminding me of
these lines, and many others equally appropriate, and beautiful
of our dear John; the Horse chesnut Trees or as they are here
called the "Buckeyes" (named I presume from the resemblance
of its fruit to the beautiful large dark brown eye of the deer)
are now so large in leaf as to tint the woods with green, the
orchards which are numerous and extensive are in richest
blossom, pink and white, Peaches Apples and Cherries, some
blue grass we have sown round the House and along the walks
of the Garden is about an inch out of the Ground, and our
vegetables are coming forward rapidly, keeping pace with your
spring, we are generally about a month earlier. With the excep-
tion of the blue bird resembling in shape and habits the robin,
we have nothing musical in the feathered tribe to usher in the
spring, no blackbird, thrush, linnet Goldfinch, or earliest
Cuckoo; our woods ring with the harsh cries of innumerable
woodpeckers of gaudy plumage and ungraceful form, but no
tender Nightingale sings his melodious song. We sometimes see
at an enormous height a flight of Swans, flying in the form of a
wedge, after the manner of ducks and Geese; Storks and cranes
of very large size frequently fish in the shallow water of the falls
within sight of the House, and when hunting in solitary places

I have seen most noble eagles. When in England this season used to elevate my spirits promising pleasant Summer,—but now it is only agreeable in itself promising long sultry days and perhaps sickness, this spring being very backward ⟨promises⟩ is however esteemed favorable to health, you shall hear as the season advances how we get on.[2]—I wrote the accompanying letter intending to send it, as it expresses by the post, but hearing Mr Briggs[3] would soon start for London I have delayed it for that opportunity; had I thought it possible he would have waited so long it should have gone as originally intended. You may fairly accuse me for not writing so frequently as I ought to have done, but I am persuaded you have not received several letters that I have sent, I hope in future that our correspondence will be attended with better fortune, I regret Miss Brawne should have been in the way of your writing to me, that letter had it come to hand would have releived me from many unpleasant feelings about you. Knowing John's affection for that young Lady I feel very much disposed to like her, altho' I was informed by persons I very much respect[4] that she was an artful bad hearted Girl, all I saw to object to in her was an appearance of want of affection for her Sister and respect for her Mother. I sincerely hope she is not connected in the change you contemplate "in your present mode of life for one more congenial to your age."[5] If you have occasion to consult any one on so delicate a step as a change of life, I presume you mean a change of residence, let me recommend Mrs Dilke to you, she has good sense and a large fund of disinterested good nature. Pray my dear Girl write more fully on this subject and do not decide if you can possibly help it without my concurrence. I am fully persuaded from the affectionate manner in which Mr Abbey mentions you that he is deeply interested in your happiness, and knowing him to be a straightforward, candid man, I feel easy while you are under his protection, and hope you will never leave it untill you change your name or live with me. I would not by any means recommend you to remain contented with being miserable any where, but I

know from experience that we can more easily see the disagree-
ables than the advantages of our present situation, a change
might possibly be for the worse. One thing is most positive, do
not intrust any one but Mr Abbey with your property,[6] nor lay
yourself under material obligations, or you will soon become the
dupe of the designing and crafty, at present this may appear
worldly minded advice, but a very few years will show you such
behaviour is necessary to a generous spirit always inclined to
overpay obligations.—Never fear in future about putting me to
the expense of postage, altho' I am not in opulent I am in easy
circumstances, and am willing to pay it whenever you have any
thing to communicate.—

The Harp is a delightful instrument and depends for its
attractions more than any instrument but the violin on the taste
and skill of the musician. I sincerely hope you may conquer it
and having so powerful a restorative at command you may at
pleasure drive away those melancholy fits you are subject to, in
fact you must be provided with some elegant accomplishment
before we come to England to help to polish your beautiful
neices from their Kentucky rust. I am sure Fanny you have not
a sallow Complexion, pale but not sallow, air and exercise only
are wanting to give you your natural colour. Your face is decidedly not spanish, but English all over.[7] If I fancied you to
resemble Don Quixote I should fancy a handsome intelligent
melancholy countenance, with something wild but benevolent
about the eyes, a lofty Forehead but not very broad, with finely
arched eyebrows denoting candour and generosity. He is an immense favorite of mine and I cannot help feeling angry with the
great Cervantes for bringing him into situations where he is the
laughing stock of minds so inferior to his own, it is evident he
was a great favorite of the author and ⟨that⟩ it is evident he was
tinted [8] with the chivalric spirit [9] he so wittily ridicules; [10] he is
made to speak as much sound sense, elevated morallity and true
piety, as any divine who ever wrote; if I were to meet with such
a man I should almost hate myself for laughing at his eccentrici-

ties.[11]—Tell me what Books you read and point out those parts that most forcibly arrest your attention, that I may frame such letters as may prove agreeable; I particularly desire to know if you have carefully read John's works & what impression they made, I will reserve my *opinion, observations* on his various excellencies and defects untill I can understand how far you are interested in the subject.

Mr Briggs will not return untill October therefore I beg you will write by post immediately on receipt of this, remembering it will be necessary to pay the inland postage, he will inform you before he leaves London where to send letters intended for me, I expect to receive a volume since you will have so much time and so sure an opportunity. You will find Mr Briggs a very agreeable man able to give you any information you desire about our situation looks &c. he went to school with me to Mr Clarks Endfield; he dined with us to day and nursed your little neices, who with Mrs Keats desire you to accept their kisses and their love. Mrs K is extremely anxious to see you and I hope the time is not very, very far distant when you will be thoroughl{y} acquainted with each other, I see you have a very high opinion of her, but {I am} persuaded it will improve still more when you become intimately acqu{ainted} with her singleness of heart, generosity, and candour, she is the antipodes of m{e,} to name all her good qualities would be but a vague description, since every person has some claim to all the virtues, but it is the graceful manner with which they are excercised that gives them their great charm. If I had the eloquence of Scott I would make her the heroine of a novel and she would make a good one for she has faults enough to take from her Character all insipidity, she is quick in her temper, overfond of the Children, and occasionally overindulgent to your most affectionate Brother and only natural protector

George Keats.

---

[1] Slightly misquoted from *Endymion*, I.41–43.

[2] *F* omits the long passage from "I wrote the" through "give you your natural

colour." Presumably the letter from "I wrote the" to the end was written sometime in May.

[3] See 26n., below.

[4] Perhaps J. H. Reynolds and his family.

[5] See p. 69, below.

[6] Later letters in this series show how Abbey mismanaged it.

[7] Valentin Llanos was in her mind. She had met him before October 8, 1821
(*Letters of F. B.,* p. 44).

[8] *F* united.

[9] *F* spirits.

[10] *Or perhaps* redicules (*F*).

[11] *F* ends here.

-»» 6 «-

GEORGE KEATS TO FANNY KEATS

February 1 8 2 5

Address: Miss. F. M. Keats./ to the care of Richd Abbey Esqre/ Pancrass
Lane/ London./ Lord Whitworth.[1]
Postmarks: A 26 MY 26 1825; LIVERPOOL *SHIP LETTER*
Brief extracts are printed in *F,* IV, 401f.

My dear Fanny   Louisville Feby 1825

The knowledge that so many letters sent by post have
never arrived, induced me to wait till Mr Briggs was established
in New Orleans,[2] so that, a surer and less expensive communication might be established thro' him, he has however undertaken
to go to Mexico, I have resolved not to wait any longer; altho'
writing a letter that possibly may not reach its destination is so
disheartening a task that it cannot be otherwise than dull, it will
however acquaint you that we are all well, and liveing comfortably, and prosperously. I hope it may arrive safe, and grieve
that we who are so peculiarly situated in the world, without
relations, and so few Friends should have no other intercourse
than a most uncertain correspondence, to continue our knowledge of each other; but for Mr Brigg's punctuallity we might
have given each other up for ever. In a few years we may per-

haps be in nearer neighbourhood, either we must come to you, or you must come to us. If I could afford time and expense to bring you here, I would not hesitate to advise you to come and live with me, it is [a] subject of frequent chat between me, and M[rs] K, but our difficulty is to get you here, and if you should wish to go back to convey you in safety, other young ladies have surmounted those objections   perhaps a favorable opportunity may induce you to do the same. For your frequent complaints, colds, sore throats, and our Family consumption this climate is considered and I beleive correctly very favorable, the Atlantic States are much the same as England—M[rs] K has been confined with her fourth Girl,[3] we hoped for a Boy to name him after poor John, who altho' so long gone from us is constantly in our minds; his miniature over our mantel peice is partly hidden by a hyacynth in bloom; Shakespeare is next above him, Tom at the top, Beaumont and Fletcher on either side. Our other less valued pictures are Wellington and Buonaparte between the windows, and the miniature of a dog by H[y] Wylie in mezzotinto over one of the doors.—The most lively recollection I have of you relates to times which I expect you have almost forgotten, when we lived with our Grandmother at Edmonton, and John, Tom and myself were always devising plans to amuse you, jealous lest you should prefer either of us to the others, now the scene is changed, you are a woman judging of pictures, giving up the harp because you cannot satisfy your own taste, copying poetry, and moreover forgetting what you learnt at School, all proofs of womanhood incontrovertible, I beg you will pardon if former vivid recollections betray me into writing any fooleries not altogether sufficiently elevated to address to my Sister Fanny at the age of maturity. I am very much gratified to hear that Miss Brawne is an amiable Girl and that eccentricity has deceived my informants into the beleif that she is unworthy, few things could give me more pleasure than to hear that the Lady of my dear Friend and Brother John's choice should be worthy of him. I trust I shall never forget M[rs] & Miss B.'s devoted attention to him during his sickness, their kindness to you encreases my debt. When I heard of John's death I reproached myself for having left one so sensitive and hypochondriacal to the bare world, when I perhaps was the only person in it who knew him well enough, who was fitted to relieve him of its friction, who was qualified to make things go easy with him. I cannot help thinking that he might now be living if I had remained with him, it is however no little consolation to me and honorable to his Friends that he should have met with so many perseveringly [4] disinterested services at every point that he needed them.—I would write something about his works if I had room, I will now only thank you for sending his last volume, his talents have honoured our name, his excellencies are written in our hearts.—What Follows is a part of a letter to Mr Abbey [5] that will be forwarded at about the same time as this, please to communicate it to him—

My dear Sir —

When I last wrote to you I had come to the understanding that the notes I had given to Taylor & Hessey thro' Tallant of Cincin^a in liquidation of their claim on John's estate, should be forwarded immediately to T & H and that they should be given up to you on your paying their acc. Mr Tallant not having attended to the business at that time, has since determined that he will not forward them, but requires me to renew them in one note that he may send it on for collection. the laws of this State are such that it would be imprudent to accede to such an arrangement, it would give Tallant a more summary mode of collecting   I have so worsted him in some letters that have passed between us, that I {would} rather not trust him with the power to hurt me. Since he will not forw{ard the} original notes you will oblige me by settling Taylor & Hessey's account, and taking their order on Tallant for the *6 notes I gave him in settlement of their account with my Brother,* as well as an indemnification, or some writing to secure me should any accident occur to prevent me from getting the notes,   I leave to you to devise the

best plan to obtain that object, I have Tallant's written engagement to give them up to T & H's order. Your letter by Briggs
asks for authority to pay Taylor & Hessey 159£—Haslam 50,—
Brown 70£ and the Taylor 30£ or 40£—I hereby request you to
pay those persons, mindg. to take such receipts as your prudence
may deem sufficient. This list amts to more than I supposed was
forthcoming, you will oblige me much by informing me when
   T & H's
you send the *order* what has been done for the others. Please to
forward duplicates one addressed to me via New York, the
other to the care of Gordon & Forstall—New Orleans.—and still
further deserve the good wishes of Dear Sir

Yours sincerely
Geo Keats.

[1] The name (written with a different pen and perhaps by another hand) of
the earl who died on May 13, 1825, aged seventy-two, though why it should be
in this address is not clear to me.

[2] In an 1827 directory he is listed as a merchant and négociant at 23 Toulouse
Street, New Orleans (*KC* I, 283 n.).

[3] Isabel: see the next letter.

[4] *Written* perseveningly.

[5] See the next letter.

→»» 7 «←-

GEORGE KEATS TO RICHARD ABBEY
18 March 1825[1]

Address: Richd Abbey Esqre/ Pancras Lane/ London
Postmarks: SHIP LETTER LIVERPOOL; F 2 JY 2 1825

Richd Abbey Esqre ⎱   Louisville March 18th 1825
    London   ⎰

My dear Sir

When I last wrote to you I had come to the understanding that the notes I had given to Taylor & Hessey, thro their agent Ja^s Tallant [2]—Cincinnati—in liquidation of their claim on John, should be forwarded immediately to Taylor & Hessey, to be given up to you on your paying their account. Tallant not having attended to the business at that time, has since determined that he will not forward them, but requires me to renew them in one note that he may send it on for collection; such an arrangement would be imprudent, since it would enable Tallant to pursue a more summary mode of collection by law, than is possible under the present circumstances; I have so worsted him in some letters that have passed between us, that I fear he has some resentment, and is prepared to give me some trouble; since he will not forward the original notes I shall be obliged by your settling Taylor & Hessey's account, and taking their order on Tallant for the 6 notes taken from me, in payment of that account, with an indemnification, or some Instrument to secure me, should any accident prevent me from getting the notes; I will leave to you to adopt the best plan to obtain that object, I have Tallant's written engagement to give them up to T & H's order.[3]

In a former letter I desired you to pay to the full in your hands all claims against John's estate, since however your last per Briggs asks for authority to pay

Taylor & Hessey	159£
Haslam	50£
Brown	70£
and the Taylor	30£ or 40£

I hereby again request you to pay those persons, being careful to take such receipts as your prudence may suggest—This list amounts to more than I supposed was forthcoming, you will oblige me by mentioning when you send Taylor & Hessey's order on Tallant for the notes, what you have been able to do for the others. Please to send duplicates one addressed to me, via New York, the other to the care of Gordon & Forstall New Orleans.[4]—I am sorry you defered writing untill you no longer had time to tell me some London news, Are Hodgkinson, Frith, Parker, Beilby, Wilkinson [5] succeeding in the world, John lent the latter 40£ or 50£, perhaps the money Could be got by application.—Give my love to Fanny I will write to her in a few days.

I hope to be able to inform you in July next that our grist Mill mentioned in a former letter is grinding 70 Barrels of Flour per 24 hours, the Saw Mill is doing well and is the main Instrument in enabling us to complete the other, which when finished will be inferior to none in the Western Country: I had need be making something for my fourth Girl was born on the 28th Feb[y],[6] I must give one of them the education of a Boy.—My best respects to M[rs] & Miss Abbey and accept for yourself the gratefull thanks of

My dear Sir.

Your sincere well wisher

Geo Keats.

[1] Part of this letter, which presumably Fanny turned over to Abbey, is loosely quoted in that preceding.

[2] For George's dealings with Taylor and Hessey, his brother's publishers, and James Tallant, see *KC* I, 214–216.

[3] On August 17, 1828, Charles Wylie asked Taylor and Hessey to send his sister, Mrs. George Keats, an order on Tallant "to give up the Bill or Bills now

in his possession drawn by" them on George, "the amount having been paid by Mr Abbey." Tallant refused to return a draft for £150 which Taylor and Hessey had made on George, February 17, 1821, and which George had refused to accept, and eventually it passed into the hands of Charles Brown and Richard Woodhouse (*KC* I, 216, 317).

[4] Merchants, négociants, 105 Royal Street, New Orleans, in 1824 and 23 Toulouse Street in 1827 (*KC* I, 283 n.).

[5] All these persons except Parker are mentioned in Fanny Keats's letter of May 31, 1826, to George (*KC* I, 297–300). I have no information about him, Frith, or Beilby. Hodgkinson was Abbey's junior partner whom Keats heartily disliked (*Letters*, pp. 375f., 498). Wilkinson was presumably the lawyer of 13 New North Street, Red Lion Square, to whom Keats presented a copy of his 1817 *Poems* (now in the New York Public Library) inscribed "to C. Wilkinson from the Author."

[6] The exact date of Isabel's birth has not elsewhere been given. She died on October 29, 1843 (*KC* I, xcvii–ci).

$$\text{→≫ } 8 \text{ ≪←}$$

GEORGE KEATS TO FANNY KEATS
5 June 1825

Address: Miss Keats./ at Rich[d] Abbey Esq[re's]/ 4 Pancrass Lane/ London
Postmarks: LIVERPOOL SE 1 1825 206; A 3 SE 3 1825
Three sentences are printed in *F*, IV, 407.

Louisville June 5th 1825 [1]

My dear Fanny

It is so short a time since I sent a long letter that you must permit me to plead continual, harrassing occupation as an excuse for the breifness of this: the necessity to overlook the Carpenters, and Millwrights engaged in erecting the Flour Mill, and attending to the Saw Mill now in its busiest season, keeps me constantly on my legs so that when I come home at night I am too much fatigued to write, and we have only till tomorrow night to make up our Packets. I will request M[r] Whittingham [2] who has resided here as long as we have to call, and see you, and acquaint you where to send letters for him to bring back, he is a worthy, good natured Fellow, but we are not very intimate, he will be able to

tell you how we look—I have written about 14 days since [3] to
M[r] Dilke who I presume will give me all information about
John's works &c, but I should be glad to receive from you any
information that may come in your way, I will repeat the request made in my last [4] to forward a copy of Shelley's "Adonais
An Elegy on John" I will write to M[r] Dilke a few words. Send
a long letter per Whittingham and let it be the picture of your
Soul, describe all your actions, occupations, thoughts, vexations,
& amusements, begining with Sunday morning and ending
with Saturday night: whenever you feel disposed, write, so that
if I am not to see you for many years I may feel one so dear to me
exists in a certain palpable character, understanding me and
being understood by me, not leave me to think that you are
distinguished only as a petticoated human being, tall, and thin,
at present I imagine you to resemble poor Tom in Features,
Person, and disposition. We are all well Father, Mother, Georgiana Emily, Rosalind, Emma Frances, and Isabel, all but the
latter send kisses and love. M[rs] K talks of coming to England on
a visit, but she must wait untill I can spare the large sum necessary for her to travel in comfort, she wishes much to see you, and
I cordially wish we were accessible enough for you to try how
you would like to live with us, you could not fail to love her; for
she is the very spirit of candour, and generosity, a cheerful companion and persevering Freind thro' good and ill, she has considerable natural talents but is not overburthen'd with accom-
plishments, and to wind up, *she is a Lady* in the best sense of the
word, and yet no Faults, yes a few, she thinks me better and
wiser than I am, she is quick in her temper, and has not the
talent to keep the children in good discipline leaving all the
chastizing to their indolent Father, and interfering when I find
chastisment necessary.—Present my respects to M[rs] & Miss
Brawne, and say I should be most happy to hear from the latter
if it is only to give me a description of her present self, and you,
when I saw her last I remember a young artist complimented
her on her having [5] revived [a] [6] tasty headdress of the age of

Charles the 2nd. I presume her sister is now a ful{l} blown Beauty. Give my respects to M^r M^{rs} and Miss Abbey. I have written to Mr Abbey [7] requesting him to settle all accounts against John to the amount of funds in his hands, I here repeat it without particulars that no opportunity may be missed to give such directions.—

Beleive me Your very affectionate Brother
            and Friend
                        Geo Keats.

[1] *The month is changed from* May.

[2] Perhaps Charles Whittingham who resided on Fifth Street between Market and Jefferson streets.

[3] He seems to refer to his letter of April 20 (*KC* I, 283–292).

[4] Before April 20 (*KC* I, 291). Fanny copied *Adonais* from the London *Literary Chronicle,* December 1, 1822, pp. 751–754, in her letter to George of May 31, 1826 (*KC* I, 297 n.).

[5] *F* complimented her [on] having.

[6] *Written* to.

[7] See the preceding letter.

⇢≫ 9 ≪⇠

GEORGE KEATS TO FANNY KEATS DE LLANOS
4 March, 1 5 April 1 8 2 6

Address: Miss F. M. Keats/ to the care of Chas Dilke Esqre/ Navy pay Office/ Sommerset House. *Readdressed by Dilke*: M^{rs} L'lanos/ Boxsted/ Downshire Hill/ Hampstead [1]
Postmark: 10 F NOON 10 3 AU 1826; TP Pimlico

Louisville March 4th 1826

My dear Fanny

I am sorry my unlimited confidence in Mr Abbey should in any measure lead to your present difficulties with him, of which I had not received the slightest hint untill the arrival of Dilke's exposée of a twelvemonth's urgings and evasions. Indeed my dear Sister you must consider me widely estranged from you when you battle twelve months in difficulties which I of all

others may be supposed to be best acquainted with—you do not
ask either advice or sympathy. I have no jealousy of those you
have consulted who are men of sense and honor—I should have
recommended them and have entreated their advice and assistance, still I may fairly feel hurt that you did not think it worth
while to communicate with me from the beginning: It is possible
that you are but slightly attached to me, remembering little of
the time when you were my pet, that you do not recollect
enough of me to love me, being but young when we were much
together—The few lines I have received from you at distant
intervals obliterated these ideas that have occasionally beset me
but your silence on this important occasion makes me feel myself forgotten. Whatever may be your feelings now, I am sure
the time will come when you will think me your best Friend—
I will however hope that you *have* written, that your letters have
miscarried, that at the same time that you had the spirit to de-
mand a settlement with Mr Abbey you wrote to acquaint me
with his probable dishonesty; thro' my ignorance of his circumstances and the extent of my claim on the court of Chancery I
have risqued and I fear lost all by giving him my power of
attorney to act for me.[2] I have written to Mr Dilke on this subject
and appointed Rice & Reynolds to act for me professionally—
Yes I am so anxious to remove all blame from you that I will
beleive you have thought of me altho' from causes beyond your
controul I have failed to receive evidence of it.—

Mr Abbey's account of your property of which Mr Dilke has
furnished me a Copy, is evidently a rough draft from his memory
to say the best of it, his ingenuity has discovered errors that
I with my present means of examination should have passed un-
noticed altho' when pointed out appear to me in the same light
as they do to him. I have no doubt I could ferret out the exact
truth if I were in London and would come if I thought all could
be obtained by merely ascertaining what is due, but to know our
rights under the present circumstances is but a small advance
towards obtaining them, in doing which I do not see wherein I

should be more effective than your present active Friends. My
business is so extensive and so entirely depends on my superintendence for its successful carrying on, that nothing short of a
certainty that my coming would be extensively useful to you or
to myself would induce me to injure myself so considerably as
to leave it. I feel that if my health is good that I cannot fail by
close attention to reallise an independance, having bought on
good terms and an accomodating credit the whole of the Mills
but one tenth, which I hope to obtain in a few weeks. Should the
business continue as productive as it is at present which I have
every reason to beleive will be the case, I shall be out of debt in
2 years and own unincumbered property, the rents of which
would support my Family without any exertion on my part.
Mr Dilke says you are well and that you will inform me fully
about your disgust at the usage you have met with at Abbey's.
I am anxiously looking out for letters and hope to receive
answers to the many letters I have formerly sent.—Are you acquainted with Reynolds sisters married & single? what sort of
women are they now? they were favorites of mine—particularly
Marian, is she the one Married? [3] Are you intimate with Miss
Brawne? what is her present character? What other Friends
have you?—Give me some account of yourself—I fear you are
moping and melancholic or you would have found your cheerful
Brother more attractive. Mrs K and myself frequently talk about
you, imagining plans to bring you out and what sort of Life you
could lead with us, if I could point out any feasible way of trans-
portation I would urge you to come and spend a year, a few
years, or a life with us as you please, should your wishes point
the same way you may possibly find out some respectable emi-
grating Family who would give you the necessary protection.
Should this business with Mr Abbey draw me to London and
my circumstances at the same time will permit I shall bring Mrs
K with me whose liveliness will charm you to return with us.
I don't like this boarding out,[4] in most cases it generates bad
feelings; you pay for what you have and do not feel thankful for

good entertainment, you feel dissatisfied when badly attended to, they bear with your Company whether disagreeable or otherwise for the sake of your Cash, and feel your presence as intrusion at times when under other circumstances they would be glad to see you. This way of living is destructive of the kindly feelings, it does not excercise them, they become palsied from inactivity—my not uncomfortable House should be your Home, you have no connections or Friends but such as the eminent talents of Poor John raised to you, and which respect to his memory continue to you, therefore my House is your Home. Do you ever laugh I have not seen you so undignified since you were not bigger than your neice Georgiana, I cannot help thinking you are uncommonly serious. Mirthful or serious I will ask the question—have you reached twenty two without an entanglement, without a wish to change your name to operate against a visit to this far countree—speak plainly I am your Father bald at all times, serious on important occasions and withall 29 years old on the 1st of March last.[5] Tell me I say joking apart if you are free heart and hand, that I may not calculate on building with preengaged materials.

By the time this arrives you will have got all your property out of the Hands of Mr Abbey, or at least have ascertained the amount you are likely to get; write to me by return of Mr Turner [6] or should he by any chance not communicate with you, by post soon after the receipt of this, all about it, as well as what you can learn about my prospects concerning the Chancery Money.

April 15th 1826—Since writing the foregoing with the view of filling up when Mr Turner had resolved when to start, we have suffered the agony of attending the sick bed, and eventually the death bed, of our dear Rosalind, our second born.[7] I presume that like all other People we shall in a short time become reconciled to our loss, altho' we think there was something *peculiar* in our child, to leave a more decided, a deeper impression on the memory than most children of her age, even than her elder sister Georgiana. She had suffered so much sickness, had been so much indulged by us, she had no pleasure out of our society, she calculated with expectation of pleasure on my being at home at meal time, met me at the door and repayed all the *immense* trouble she imposed on us by an evident strength of affection that is unfelt by most children, and I think by our others. She was exquisitely beautiful, and the admiration of the whole town, whose sympathy justifies us in our opinion of her. I built much on her affectionate disposition being a Family link to hold her more volatile sisters together in bond of amity when we are no longer with them or when we are too old to influence their affections. She is however gone with all her charms real or imaginary, and our sorrow should be and perhaps is mitigated by the knowledge that her tender constitution would not in all probability have lasted to maturity, that we must have lost her at some future time when she will have engrafted herself still more firmly in our hearts, and moreover that her indulged, tender, reserved disposition was not calculated to make her happy in nine tenths of the situations that fall to the lot of mortals.—All left of us are Well, M^rs K—Georgiana, and Emma send their love. Isabel was one year old on the first of March; she has only four teeth and can neither walk nor talk.—

My best rem^s to the Dilke's & the Reynolds'es,

> who am
>
> > Your affectionate Brother
> >
> > George Keats.

[1] An address not before associated with the Llanoses, who were married on March 30.

[2] See *KC* I, 298; 300f., and p. 39, below.

[3] Eliza Reynolds married George Longmore in 1822; Jane, Thomas Hood in 1825. Marian (e) married H. G. Green later on—sometime before 1833.

[4] She had been living with a Mr. and Mrs. Lewis, Beaufort Row, Chelsea (Adami, p. 123). Probably she moved from the Abbeys' still earlier, for Gerald Griffin (*The Life of Gerald Griffin. By His Brother* [Dublin, n.d.], p. 146) wrote to his sister on June 21, 1825: "I think it probable I may some of these days become acquainted with the young sister of poor Keats the poet, as she is coming to spend some time with a friend of mine."

[5] George was born on February 28, 1797. He and his family seem to have thought March 1 his birthday, and his original tombstone in Western Cemetery, Louisville (see the Louisville *Commercial*, November 2, 1860, and *KC* I, civ n.), bore the date March 1, 1798. (Other writers, like J. A. Piatt, as quoted in *Every Saturday*, December 30, 1871, p. 635, and F. J. Koch, in the *South Atlantic Quarterly*, XXIII [1924], 163f., give the date as March 1, 1778.)

[6] On Turner, see *KC* I, 300f.

[7] Born December 18, 1821 (see p. 15, above). The date of her death has not before been known.

·» 10 «·

L. MANNING TO FANNY KEATS DE LLANOS

9 April 1826

Address: Mrs Llanos/ 4 Michael's Grove/ Brompton [1]
Postmark: 4 EVEN 4 10 AP 1826

Walthamstow
April 9th

My dear Fanny/

Quite unexpectedly I received directions from home on Sunday [2] last to set off for England on the following Morning which annoyed me exceedingly—I arrived in London at ½ past eight on Wednesday evening and leave for Ireland tomorrow morning at an early hour [3] I have been staying with the Marchioness of Ormonde [4] at the Burlington Hotel and yesterday the *first leisure time* I had I endeavoured to see you—I had great difficulty in finding you and after all was disappointed—I congratulate you on your change of name and state may it prove a happiness to you is the sincere wish of your affectionate friend—When I heard it was a Spaniard you were married to I concluded it [5] was the Gentleman I once saw at Mr Dilke's but on an interview with the Gentleman I soon [6] perceived my mistake—I was before afraid you had tied yourself to old age What I have *seen* of your husband I like your choice and I hope in every respect you may have cause to rejoice in it—I suppose

you have of late had so much on your mind that you could not
devote your time to an absent friend but I forgive you as I know
little or nothing of the anxiety love occasions previous to matri-
mony and it may be *excessive*—I shall expect to hear from you
when I reach home which will be in a week and write to me
when you get to the Continent   you know my address—With
Comp^ts to Mr Llanos I remain

My dear Fanny

Your Sincere and Affectionate Friend

L Manning [7]

PS   I do not know how to spell your name   excuse all imper-
fections for I am in great has[t]e

Yours ever

LM

[1] A previously unrecorded address for the Llanoses.

[2] April 2.

[3] If she did so, this letter was posted after she left London.

[4] Louisa Grace, daughter (died 1860) of John Staples, wife of James Butler
(1774–1838), who was created fifth marquess on October 5, 1825.

[5] *Written* it it.

[6] Followed by a period.

[7] A woman friend not mentioned by any writer on the Keatses.

⇢⟫ I I ⟪⇠

GEORGE KEATS TO FANNY KEATS DE LLANOS

23 May 1827

Address: Mr Goodacre/ 72 St Pauls Church Yard/ Mrs Llanos (care of) /
Chas Dilke Esqre./ Navy Pay Office/ Sommerset House/ London

My very dear Sister   Louisville ⎫
                             Kentucky ⎬ May 23rd 1827

A Mr Goodacre [1] who has been lecturing in every princi-
pal city in the Union on astronomy will be here in a few
minutes to dine with us, & will start immediately after dinner
for England direct, on learning which I directly set down to

inform you of my existence. I have not had any conversation with him since he left this place four months since, therefore do not know if it will be convenient for him to seek you out, and give you some idea by word of mouth of our looks and manner of living, should he call, please to extend to him every politeness in your pow{er.} I have been sorely disappointed at not hearing from you so long, particularly as I had promised myself on receiving your last a very frequent intercourse; you surrounded by numerous friends may not feel the solitude of living with affections shut up and confined within the narrow boundaries of a family circle; but for the stimulating occupation of business I should become a misanthrope out side of my own doors, I therefore desire, ardently desire a continued intercourse with one who engaged my fraternal affections at a time when she did not know, was not alive to the value of such affections The friendliness and kindly feeling which you have taught me to feel for M[r] Llanos should not be chilled by so cold a silence, if in his intercourse with me, he may not meet with cultivated intellect, he may depend upon kind, hearty brotherly Friendship that circumstances cannot alter. Convey to him my best regards. I have read his freemason [2] and felt warmed by its liberallity and noble feeling, may that and all his other productions succeed with the world to the utmost of his wishes, all I would ask, would be that they be fairly appreciated. I am anxiously looking for M[r] Turner [3] expecting letters by him since so long a period since his arrival in England has passed without hearing from you by the post, he is expected in June, if he does not bring letters I despair hearing from you any more. Not knowing your address I am constrained to trouble M[r] Dilke with this, convey to him my thanks for his many kindnesses, which have proved as valuable to me, as they have been costly to him in time and patience. My warmest rem[s] to M[rs] Dilke. After Turner's arrival whether he bring letters or not I will write to all—I have not yet heard from

Rice & Reynolds to whom I have addressed several letters, and fear much they have not come to hand, or their answers are miscarried—circumstances made it possible they might have remitted me some money, so that it is material that I should be made acquainted soon if they have received my Power of Attorney &c,[4] or if indeed there is such a Firm as Rice & Reynolds to which address my communications have been sent. I feel ashamed of urging so frequently my wish to hear about the progress of Mr Abbey's affairs, I cannot help hoping for something from that quarter, or allowing such hopes to influence [5] my arrangements in a manner that I fear will bring upon me some trouble. All that I have heard of the business was from Mr Dilke whose last letter was dated 28th July 1826.

Let me hear from you very soon, and endeavour to give me some idea of the manner in which you live, with whom and what sort of people you cheifly associate, I sincerely hope M^{rs} K and myself will one day form part of the Friendly circle—She desires her love to you—Our three Girls are pretty well in health, altho all of us have suffered some sickness this winter. Beleive me My dear Fanny

Your affectionate Brother
Geo Keats

[1] Compare *Outline of Eight Lectures on Astronomy, and of an Introductory Lecture,* an announcement of lectures Robert Goodacre gave at Washington Hall, New York, in May and June, 1825. His *Arithmetic* (1803) reached a ninth edition in 1839. The signature and the St. Paul's address are probably in his hand.

[2] That is *Sandoval* (see p. 52, below).

[3] See p. 34, above.

[4] Sent before October 18, 1826 *(KC* I, 301).

[5] *Changed from* from influencing.

GEORGE KEATS TO FANNY KEATS DE LLANOS

2 5 March 1 8 2 8

Address: W W at Messrs Gattie and Peirce's/ 57 New Bond Street [1]

Louisville March 25th 1828.

My dear Sister.

It is now nearly two years since I heard from you,[2] in which time I have written thrice—I will not trouble you with my inferences—It was my intention to have waited the departure of a Gentleman who is going to London before I dispatch'd another letter, this is now sent in consequence of an event mentioned below, and I expect M[rs] Keats will deliver the next herself, her visit to London being hastened by the necessity that I should have some one there to settle my business. She would not otherwise have gone untill 1829 when I might possibly have accompanyed her.

M[r] Rice wrote to me on the 5th April 1827 stating that such and such sums were forthcoming requiring powers &c to collect them amounting to upwards of £500 and asking in what way he should remit the money, I drew for 350£ at 90 days sight, he accepted the dft but failed to pay it when at maturity and it is now here to be taken up by me swelled in amount 20 per Cent besides expences. His change of residence coupled with this failure to pay an accepted dft looks very like bankrupcy, I sincerely hope for his & Reynolds sake as well as mine that this is not the case, but it looks like it, and should it be so, and should you have been acquainted with it, knowing that I employed them, I shall feel very sorely your neglect in not writing to me. Indeed you should have written at all events.—The apparently dangerous situation of my affairs therefore makes it necessary that I should be in London, since however my business here renders such an absence almost impossible I shall have to depend on

what Mrs Keats can do. Mr Rice has given me a statement of my
account with you & Mr Llanos wherein it appears that you fall in
my debt £7.18.7 money, and £341.11.9 Stock, and that you held
a mortgage on property of Mr Abbey's ⟨to the⟩ in which I am
interested to the amount of £267.12.0. If you have not paid over
to Rice the above, or have any left unpaid, please to consult
Dilke before you do pay it, who will know the situation of M^r
Rice.³ You will much oblige me by writing immediately as well
about this affair as yourself, and Mr Llanos, & child. I will write
again by M^rs K or the Gentleman spoken of.

My respects to Mr Llanos and love to the little Black eyed
Llanos, you see I hear *of* you altho' not *from* you — and am
                    Your affectionate Brother
                         Geo Keats.

Not knowing your address I shall enclose this to Mr H^y Wylie,
my surmises about R & R'. insolvency may be incorrect, therefore it will be evident to you that nothing should be spread
about it, that purely originates in those surmises.
                         Geo Keats.

¹ Gattie and Peirce were perfumers and comb-makers. The address is not in
George's hand. I cannot explain "W W" unless it is an error (see the postscript) for
"H. W." or refers to some other Wylie.
² Presumably since her letter of May 31, 1826, announcing her marriage
(*KC* I, 297–300).
³ For a letter on these details that George wrote to Dilke also on March 25
see *KC* I, 310–312.

                    ⇛ 13 ⇚

GEORGE KEATS TO FANNY KEATS DE LLANOS¹
              June (?) 1 8 2 8

My dear Sister/ It is with much pleasure I address you
"*my dear Sister,*" under the assurance that such expression of
my affection for you will be received by you with joy and satisfaction; for 2 years or more so far from feeling that confidence

I doubted if my letters would be received with common welcome. After so long an absence of letters from you I became
puzzled to find excuses for your apparent neglect, and must
acknowledge that I had settled into the beleif [2] that you were
careless of my correspondence, and that I had lost my Sister. I
had fears of a different nature which I bury with a disbeleif of
the existence of what I feared. I am glad that I desired M^r
Wylie to call on you, for it will be the means of assuring M^rs
Keats that she will be welcome to your hearth, who started from
home doubting the cordiallity of her reception. She is the bearer
of a letter to you.–She is now with you,[3] you are beginning to
know her, I hope before you part, you will form a good opinion
of each other, and that your meeting will be the means of
forming a secure foundation for a lasting correspondence, co-
equal with our lives, in whatever quarter of the world we may
live. You advise me to come and reside in England, I do not
want the inclination, but at present the change would be impossible. The letter I addressed to you on the 25th March [4]
should have been written to Mr Llanos had I known he was not
averse to my correspondence. —— You write now with the confidence of a woman, there is not that restraint on your pen there
was formerly, I should very much like to be acquainted with
your present self–George [5] must watch you closely and paint
you to me with the faithfulness of a flemish artist, she has a
talent that way, and is not very apt to leave in the back ground
what there may be in the picture that is rediculous. You must
not fail to tell me every particle of what you think of her, I can
bear to hear anything. You call me such "a considerate, good
natured fellow," look you then now, are you not confident?–I
am not a good natured fellow, I used to be so both in fact and
appearance, but now I am less so in fact, and if I may judge from
the almost universal fear (or something like it) that People have
of me, less so in appearance. I am envelloped in an atmosphere
⟨of⟩ whether of pride, or reserve, or ill nature or all or neither,
that keeps People at a distance. Mrs Keats indeed has no fear of

me, she dares do any thing to the non descript, even to the endeavouring to tell as near as may be what I am. Present my best wishes to Mr Llanos and say I will write to him as soon as I can learn the particulars about the wine and brandy trade.—I am much pleased that he considers himself one of the family, and it shall not be either the fault of my will or negligence if he becomes dissatisfied with me—I will explain to him the reasons why I cannot think of changing my residence at present. You say you have been to the continent,[6] to what part of it? and what sojourn did you make? tell me all about it. Welcome with a kiss, not "a thousand," my neice Irené to my relationship, of whose dark eyes I long since heard thro' Mr H^y Wylie—Tell me what you think of Georgiana [7]—Her eyes are of the first water, the upper part of her Face good; but the lower part requires to be in repose; I hope her journey and residence among you will improve her manners. Kiss our only light eyed one, our boy John, "John Keats" I wish he had as much of poor John in his face as Georgiana has.[8] Beleive me my very dear Fanny

Your most affectionate Brother George.

[1] An oblong slip probably cut off a letter (perhaps that following) to some other correspondent.

[2] *Written* befeif. *In the next sentence, too, he originally wrote* disbefeif.

[3] She sailed for New York around May 12 (*KC* I, 313).

[4] The preceding letter.

[5] His wife Georgiana.

[6] They went to Paris in August, 1826. Adami (p. 125) thinks they remained there till about September, 1828; but the letters herewith printed show that they were back at Wentworth Place, Hampstead, at least by June, 1828.

[7] His daughter.

[8] Emma Keats (Mrs. Philip) Speed wrote to Fanny Llanos on April 1, 1863, that John was "an eccentric unbalanced genius [who] wanders we know not whither." In his later years he was surveyor and bridge commissioner of De Kalb County, Missouri. See Rollins, *Harvard Library Bulletin*, IV (1950), 244f., 247. He lived until 1917.

→» 14 «←

GEORGE KEATS TO VALENTIN LLANOS

1 0, 1 1 July 1 8 2 8

Address: Mr V. Llanos./ Wentworth Place/ Downshire Hill/ Hampstead
near/ London. [*At the left in another hand:*] Deu/ Devonshire Hill
Postmarks: 7 NIGHT 7 4 SP 1828; TP BgeSt Lamb^th

My dear Sir   Louisville July 10th 1828.

It was with great pleasure that I received your's and my
sister's wedded letters, which were not the less acceptable from
being altogether unexpected. I will not conceal from you that
I considered myself forgotten by my Sister, and entirely lost
sight of by you; the possibility of miscarriage of letters was the
staff on which I leaned, but latterly that staff failed me, and
hope almost expired. At the very extremity however your letters
have started into life not only a healthy hope, but a certainty
that a pleasureable intercourse will be kept up between us; I
doubt not to our mutual gratification, certainly to mine. Immediately on the receipt of your's I wrote to my Sister in a
letter to Mrs Keats of the 1st July.—[1]

Altho' only 2 1 when I left England my character, manners,
and habits were so completely formed, that my long residence in
this country has failed to wean my mind from English associations as the most agreeable, or to give it that American tone
which seems to have become engrafted on that of all my countrymen, who have been so long and so early exposed to the effects
of the circumstances and opinions that here surround them. I
feel myself an *Englishman,* and am looked upon as obstinately
such, enjoying the respect of my neighbours and acquaintances,
but unable to mix with them intimately, familiarly or un-
reservedly, whether the fault is in me or them, or both of us or
neither, they seem as conscious as I am of our unamalgamating
qualities and are likely to leave me in possession of my unpopu-
lar identity. I perhaps flatter myself in supposing that I am more

free from national prejudices than most men, what few I am stained withal are those of an Englishman which are here of all others the most unpardonable that a man can cherish. Under these circumstances it is not likely that my residence in this country is [a] matter of choice as it regards all sociable relations, and whenever my circumstances are so flourishing as to raise me above the fear of wanting the means to live respectably and liberally without the necessity of excercising a too pinching economy, I will certainly change my dwelling place, and seek a more congenial people amongst whom to cherish my sociable social virtues. At present however I am bound by my business and property to remain where I am, keeping in view a future change, and having an intention to sell whenever I can obtain a fair price. Mrs Keats will inform you in what manner we live, surrounded by ⟨plenty of⟩ numerous negroo servants [2] and superfluous plenty; maintaining a general outline of economy that will insure our expences to be within our income, but careless of those trifling expenditures that surrounded by circumstances attending a dense population would be matters of serious consideration. Our servants impose upon us without fretting us, and we with a profusion quite congenial, scatter our dollars without sighing at their disappearance. I think an english education more favorable to the morals as well as health of our children, but that they will have better prospects of living an easy after life in this country. I will take another opportunity to disscuss the feasibility of living in England, as well as several other topics that my mind now presents to me, when I have leisure, and am not bound as now to time: this is a very busy season and I am almost bewildered with over occupation. More information about the wine and Brandy trade will be forwarded to you by a friend of mine in Phl^a to whom I will write on the subject, below you will find what particulars I could gather here, where both articles are now very dull. The last congress reduced the wine duties considerably. I will request Drury [3] to explain the consequences of the change.

Be assured that your proffer of Friendship is to me matter of much joy, and that I have great pleasure in subscribing myself your Friend & Brother

Geo Keats.

Convey to Miss Brawne my kind regards, and let Irené know as soon as her intellect can comprehend that she has a loving uncle George. Kiss her little Spanish Face, acting as my proxy. G. K.

The par value of a dollar is ⁵4. ᵈ6 Stᵍ present exchange 10 ¾ per Cent in favor of London, there are 100 Cents to the dollar—Duty on spirits distilled from other materials than grain. 1ˢᵗ and 2ⁿᵈ proof 38 Cents per Gallon 3ʳᵈ proof, 42 Cents and 4ᵗʰ proof 48 Cents 5ᵗʰ proof, 57 Cents per Gallon.—Duty on Wines. Madeira, Burgundy, Rhenish, Champaigne, Tokay 100 Cents per Gallon . . . [He then gives nearly a page of further details about the prices of brandy, Rochelle, Bordeaux, Malaga, port, and the like in gallons, casks, bottles, or pipes. Among "Sales in New York. 28 June." one observes twenty dozen of "Champaigne," which brought from \$7 to \$9 per dozen. Then follows a postscript.]

July 11ᵗʰ ⁴ 1828

I have this morning received yours of the 23ʳᵈ May as well as a letter from Dilke,[5] and one from Henry Wylie—I am obliged to you for your punctuallity, and will leave Mʳˢ Keats[6] to thank you in a suitable manner. I once more subscribe myself

Your Friend and Brother

Geo Keats.

[1] Possibly the oblong slip-letter preceding, although in it he says that his wife "is the bearer of a letter" to Fanny Llanos.

[2] He had four domestic slaves at the time of his death.

[3] Michael Drury, a Philadelphia merchant and a cousin of John Taylor's (KC I, 100–102, 217–220).

[4] *Changed from* 12ᵗʰ.

[5] To which George replied on July 12 (KC I, 315–317).

[6] Who was then in England.

→» 15 «←

GEORGE KEATS TO FANNY KEATS DE LLANOS

1 2　July　1 8 2 8

Address: Mrs Llanos/ Wentworth Place/ Hampstead/ London
Postmarks: 7 NIGHT 7 4 SP 1828; TP BgeSt Lamb^th

Louisville July 12th 1828

My very dear Sister

You have already found out that I am not the considerate,
good natured fellow [1] you took me for; listen my good Sister,
and fix your opinion of me midway between the one formerly
entertained, and the present one recently expressed.—

Politely endeavouring to forstall all argument you tell me you
"know what I would say" and stifle my reasonable explanation
by an embrace to which finalé I hope however to be conducted
at last, but first hear me, harken to my tale, for Oh, woman,
woman what precious justification are you willing to leave unheard or unattended to that you may have the last word; or
were you hurt enough by my apparent censure to fear that the
act of probing the wound would encrease its irritation. Now I
have pen, ink paper, and Solitude, so you may raise your voice
to the top of its compass, or modulate it to its most entreating
tones, without stopping one syllable of my say. However much
I covet your forgiveness for having cherished suspicions of your
kindly feelings towards me, I do not desire to be sheltered
under the skreen "of irritated feelings produced by disappointment" which you have kindly spread before me. I disclaim
irritated feelings, and present as my excuse the having acted
correctly and justifyable according to my knowledge and the
means I had of judging; my feelings were wounded, mortified,
but not irritated. When I was under the impression from most
reasonable deductions that R & R [2] were bankrupt, and was
assured that that misfortune could not have befallen them

without your knowledge, it necessarily appeared to me that you
knowing that they were acting for me having in fact paid money
to them for my benefit, that you I say of all others was the person
to apprise me of my danger. Your not having answered my
urgent letters for so long a time confirmed my opinion of your
carelessness about me and my Interests, and I pray you my dear
Flesh and blood Sister place yourself for an instant in my situation and think in what manner you would have acted. I feared
that I had lost a considerable sum of money which had recently
been snatched from a wreck, from the want of a little piloting
that should have been performed by you. It all amounts to this,
that had my suppositions been true, and Dilke says I had strong
grounds for my beleif, my complaint (if I made any) ⟨was just⟩
would have been just: as however my surmises were groundless
I have the most intense pleasure in receiving into my "heart of
hearts" [3] a loving Sister, and confessing myself precipitate and
in error when I imputed to her (as I confess I did whatever my
letters expressed) want of affection for me and coldness for my
interests. So as you say "let us embrace and think no more of
the ugly letter" which I am sorry "has cost you so much
anxiety"; the cost however has not been altogether mispent,
since it has procured for me farther assurance that you have a
warm feeling of affection towards one who has so long been
forced by appearances to doubt it. I did not intend to accuse
Dilke of carelessness to my Interests, he kindly conducted our
affairs to a resting place, and then gave them up to the pro-
fessional guidance of R. & R. His name was inserted in my last
power of attorney by mistake, but I had no idea that my interests
were under his superintendance, Whatever expressions I may
have used in the course of explaining my feelings or situation,
whatever signification they may be supposed to bear were
decidedly never intended by me to reflect on the conduct of my
good and kind Friend Dilke, I flatter myself he does not think
so himself. To have applied to him at [4] all on the subject is
evidence that I did not think him careless of my Interests, by
what bond was he bound to attend to and transact my business?

he had already done enough to satisfy his friendliness—I hope this disagreeable construction has been confined to my sensitive Sister, and if it has spread further I depend on her Zeal for my good name to remove the false impression. Since I shall hear from you and your Sister George [5] so soon I will not dwell on your different capacities for loving and pleasing each other, I do most ardently desire that you may prove congenial spirits and that time has in store for you many years of pleasurable communication: I retain you as my counsel to argue against her too long stay in England, I fear you will make it too agreeable to her, her poor home will lose its attractions in comparison.

Having a multiplicity of Mill business to attend to and only short evenings to write, and even those only occasionally, and many letters to make up before the starting of M[r] John Bull [6] I am obliged to stop with requesting you to pay more than common politeness, civilities to him, whose name if he were otherwise without recommendation should be a passport to your good offices. He is a plain straightforward, worthy, uneducated, sagacious, slow minded, spirited, brave native born Kentuckian, bred a builder. He was once my travelling companion under circumstances that bring out the inside of a mans heart, and we were mutually informed thereby of each others composition, We do not associate much, not being fitted for companions, but good feeling towards each other is current to a very considerable extent, he is now engaged extensively in the Staffordshire ware Business. I am persuaded he would do much to serve me. I hope that M[rs] K will return under his protection, than whom I would not de{sire} a better guardian. Punning is his Antipodes, and yet he laughed when I trans{fixed} him with one. The Steam Boat in which we travelled was detained by ice about half way up the Mississippi, and we went out a gunning; after we were tired out with unsuccess, we desired to strike straightway for our boat, in our course we got entangled in a cane break, so high and ⟨almost⟩ so nearly impenetrable that we almost despaired of getting out of it; we were confident of our direction but the thickets [7] almost made our progress in the right course impossible; I mounted a tree about 25 or 30 Feet to look out and distinguished a somewhat less obstructed way; again we came to a stand from the same causes as before; when it was Bull's turn to climb which did not prove to him so easy as it had done to me, for he lost his wind, and for a time could neither ascend or descend, while he was in momentary fear of falling it struck me what an odd thing it was to see a Bull up in a tree, which he looked as much like as any thing else thro' the mass of foliage, when in the very midst of his trouble I cried out to him that I had heard of Bears climbing trees but I never expected to see a Bull at such an altitude. He reserved his laugh untill a short residence on terra firma had restored his breath: this was good nature. I am glad you are at Wentworth place—I can reallise the scene that surrounds you, I can see you walking about the garden, feeling a satisfaction that your jerusalems and peas, and Pinks and roses are more flourishing or productive or beautiful than your friend & neighbour Mrs B.—present my respects to that Family, I remember the ripe as well as the growing beauty,[8] and poor Sam—[9] I remember the chairs and the curtains and the cats, and the twelv⟨e⟩th cake.—I desire much to hear about Miss Brawne.—Convey to Mr Llanos assurances of my desire of becoming respected and beloved by him—and on your part beleive me

My very dear Fanny

Your most affectionate Brother

Geo. Keats

[1] See p. 42, above.
[2] Rice and Reynolds.
[3] See *Hamlet*, III. ii. 78.
[4] *Written* at at.
[5] Mrs. George Keats.
[6] John P. Bull, a Louisville merchant, of Bull, Rankin, and Leight, wholesalers, 18 East Main Street, who also (*KC* I, 316n.) carried George's letter of July 12 to Dilke.
[7] *Written* thicknets.
[8] Fanny and Margaret Brawne.
[9] Who died on March 28, 1828.

→≫ 16 ≪←

GEORGE KEATS TO FANNY KEATS DE LLANOS

5 March 1 8 2 9

Address: Mrs Llanos/ Wentworth Place/ Downshire Hill/ Hampstead
Postmarks: 12 NOON 12 23 MY 1829; 4 EVEN 4 MY 23 1829; TP Charing
Cross

My dear Sister   Louisville March 5th 1829

Mr Briggs,[1] who called on you some years ago at my
request, will be the bearer of this, either to your hand or to the
two penny post. His stay here will be so short that I have not
time to write at the length I should wish particularly as I have
to write to so many, all of which must be done by ten o'clock
to morrow morning.—Mrs Keats arrived at New York after a
passage of 33 days, I was on the beach ready to receive her, and
was happy to see her and the children look so well, they are
certainly improved by the journey. We find home most particularly comfortable after so much travelling, and so long, and
I beleive on both sides so painful a separation. She is very much
pleased with her visit, and altho' it has been very costly to me
both in feeling and purse, I am glad it is accomplished, and I
do not think the money badly expended. The main drawback
to my satisfaction is that circumstances prevented you from becoming so well acquainted with her as might reasonably have
been expected. Mr Llanos in his letter seems likewise to have
regretted it. Whatever may have been the cause, I am quite sure
that if ever you do become acquainted with her intimately, you
will greive that you have allowed this opportunity to pass un-
improved. If I should be as successful in business in the three
succeeding years as I have been in 1828, I shall pay you a visit
in 1832, and if our family is so situated as to permit it, M^{rs} K
will accompany me; affording another opportunity to cement a
relationship by Friendship, that may prove serviceable to one or
both in future and be a source of present satisfaction and en-

joyment. I am happy to hear that you are so comfortably situated at Wentworth place, and that my little neice Irene is so pretty and so engaging: Georgiana used to be both, but she is now at "the awkward age," when few children are either the one or the other. I put a letter into the Post office New York ⟨acqu⟩ for Mr C. Llanos [2] informing him where to find me in that City, but I did not hear from him. I am much pleased with Mr Llanos present of his works which I have placed by the side of John's on my favorite shelf. For the honor of human nature I hope the scenes of perfidy exhibited in them are exaggerated, altho' the manner in which they are related makes them appear so real. I had read Sandoval in the American edition. [3] When I have more time I will enlarge on this subject. I will write to Mr Llanos by a Gentleman from Bristol [4] who will pass thro' this place on his way home in a month or two: present to him my thanks and best wishes.

You have not given me any account of your visit to the continent, where did you go? what did you see?

M^rs K says you are a female edition of Tom, [5] I have a good sketch of him over my mantle and can easily reallise your looks— I am in looks about 20 years older than the likeness Severn painted of me in 1817. [6] I can perfectly understand M^r L's looks and manners from {the} description as well as those of Miss Margaret Braw{ne} assisted by what I remember of her when I was in England in 1820. Mrs Reynolds, Marianne Reynolds and Mrs Dilke sent me very kind letters which has operated with other feelings ⟨considerably⟩ to make me long for a visit to my native land; I shall certainly come when I can spare the funds without inconvenience. Mr Briggs will let you know when he intends to return that you may send letters, which opportunity I beg you will take advantage of to write to your Affectionate Brother

Geo Keats.

[1] See *KC* I, 281, 283, 319f., and pp. 22f., above.
[2] See pp. 55f., below.

[3] *Sandoval; Or, The Freemason* (2 vols., E. Bliss and E. White, Collins and Hannay, and others, New York, 1826).

[4] A Mr. Hartford (see *KC* I, 319, 332).

[5] Dilke, annotating R. M. Milnes's 1848 biography of Keats, says of Tom: "He was very like Mrs Llanos—so like that John spoke of it as most painful to him." See also *Letters*, p. 530.

[6] Severn's miniature of George, now in the Keats-Shelley House, Rome. It is reproduced in M. B. Forman's Hampstead Edition of Keats (New York, 1938), I, lxxvi.

->>> 17 <<<-

GEORGE KEATS TO FANNY KEATS DE LLANOS AND
VALENTIN LLANOS
15 November 1829

Address: Mr V. Llanos/ Wentworth Place/ Hampstead near/ London/ England/ via New York
Postmarks: LOUIS KY NOV 17; TP Rate 2; PAID; F 2 JA 2 1830; 10 NOON 10 JA 2 1830; *SHIP LETTER* LIVERPOOL

Louisville[1] Nov 15th 1829

My dear Fanny.

I congratulate you on bringing into the world my fair nephew Luis Mariano Llanos,[2] and am most happy in his acquaintance, long may he live and be a comfort and an honour to his Parents, we have within a few days been informed that Mrs Chas Wylie [3] has a boy and named him Geo Keats. In three mos I hope to be entitled to be congratulated on the birth (I hope) of another boy. Altho it is my present intention to visit England I fear if you leave for Valladolid early in the summer, I shall be too late to see you, and if I fail to see you before you go it is probable I never shall. I would not on my own account have you to leave England, the only land besides N^th America that I ever expect to visit, still I can offer no sufficient reason why you should not go wherever Mr Llanos' interest requires. The natural habit of making comparisons between our present in-

conveniences and enjoyments, ⟨and⟩ making what we have been
accustomed to, the standard of excellence is the greatest pre-
ventive of a disireable state of mind to enjoy happiness in a
foreign land: my experience teaches that the educated in all
civilized countries are nearly equally sensible and happy, misfortunes arising from war and misgovernment excepted; manners and customs arise principally from climate, we shall therefore find for the most part that however we may dislike them at
first, that our own experience will eventually pursuade us of
their appropriateness. It is likely that on reading this you will
laugh at your wise Brother, I hope it will not ⟨be⟩ take *more
than ten years* foreign residence to enable you to act up to my
ideas, if you do in five your Husband will have sufficient cause to
fall down on his Spanish knees and worship his English Non-
pareil. I hope for Mr Llanos sake that the holy Ferdinand [4] is
better advised than formerly, the portraits he has drawn of him
are not of a nature to be forgotten or forgiven. I am ignorant of
the present state of things in Spain but I know something of
human nature, and that knowledge ⟨and that knowledge⟩ would
lead me to doubt the policy of the writer of Estaban and
Sandoval [5] putting himself in the power of any official who desires the favor of the beloved monarch. His writings are not
merely the expression of political opinions but likewise personal invictive, to a vindictive and common mind unpardonable.
If Ferdinand does not revenge he is not the man the author of
those works described. Wherever you go you may be assured of
my ardent wishes for your happiness and prosperity. I do not
doubt my ability to show Dilke that his cause for displeasure
arose altogether from a very pardonable ignorance on my part
of the real state of accounts, he has proved himself in no
common way my Freind when I stood in need of one, and will
never find me forgetfull of his many favours. I have written to
him.[6] Mrs K. and children are well. Do not allow so much time
to pass without writing again. I will write a few lines to M^r

Llanos on this sheet. M^rs K desires to [be] kindly remembered.
I am

my dear Sir [7]

Your affectionate Brother

George Keats.

My dear Sir

    I am talking of visiting England as soon as I can arrange my affairs to allow of a five months absence, I cannot fix upon the time at present; I fear however that you will have departed for your native land before I can make it convenient to come, it would afford me much gratification to see you and Fanny perhaps for the last time, and I still hope that circumstances will allow that pleasure by keeping you a little longer than Fanny seems to expect. M^rs K's situation will keep me at home untill February, I hardly hope to be able to leave home in the summer, therefore next winter will be the probable time of my visit. I speak at random and as you will see without information when I express fear for your safety in Spain—you ought to know best—be assured of my anxiety for your safety prosperity and happiness. Your volumes are placed among my favorites on my shelves and present themselves to my sight daily, they will prove unfailing remembrancers of your genius and kindly feelings towards me, as the honourable manner in which you have acted in the money transactions between us will of your honorable principles. I shall read Don Estaban [8] and Sandoval and Van Halen [9] again and examine if I have cause undoubted to fear for your safety in Spain, if you have brought to public view the vices of monsters in power you may depend on receiving punishment, if they have the power to inflict it whatever they may promise of safety and forgiveness. I hope most sincerely that you will not suffer from a too great confidence in the present quiet appearance of things.—I am sorry for your Brother's misfortunes and should have been pleased to have been in any way instrumental in saving him from them [10]—It was notorious here at the time he went that the native Mexicans were violently hostile to, and suspicious of old Spain Spaniards; had he mixed much in Society he will have heard enough to have induced him to give up his purpose of going to that country. M^rs K and Georgiana desire to be kindly remembered—we are all in good health, and I am enjoyi{ng} tolerable prosperity. Do me the favour to write when you have fixed on t{he} day of your departure for Spain, and again on your arrival at your spanish home. Wishing you health happiness and prosperity I subscribe myself Your Friend & Brother

Geo Keats.

¹ Fanny *prefixed* Kentucky.

² Born July 25, 1829, died August 15, 1834.

³ Mrs. George Keats's sister-in-law.

⁴ Ferdinand (Fernando) VII, king of Spain (1784–1833).

⁵ See pp. 38, 52, 55, above.

⁶ See George's letter of November 14 to Dilke (*KC* I, 320–324).

⁷ *A slip for* Sister.

⁸ *Don Esteban; Or, Memoirs of a Spaniard. Written by Himself* (3 vols.; London, 1825).

⁹ Llanos' *Narrative of Don Juan Van Halen's Imprisonment in the Dungeons of the Inquisition at Madrid, and His Escape in 1817 and 1818* (2 vols.; London, 1827). See pp. 57f., below.

¹⁰ On May 7, 1822, Fanny Brawne (*Letters of F. B.*, p. 64) told Fanny Keats that Llanos' "brother is gone to join the independents in South America rather odd that, to fight against his own country." From George's comments it appears that this or another brother was somehow involved in the unsuccessful attempt of Spain to reconquer Mexico in 1829—an attempt crushed by Santa Anna in September.

GEORGE KEATS TO FANNY KEATS DE LLANOS
2 2 November 1 8 3 0

Address: Mrs Llanos/ Care of Messrs Reynolds & Simmons [1]/ Golden Square/ London/ Mr Cuthbertson/ 44 South Molton S^t

Louisville Nov 22nd 1830

My dear Sister

I take advantage of Mr Cuthbertson's [2] departure for London to remind you of my existence, and remembrance. I have not heard from you since you informed me that it was your intention to go to Spain last summer—I wrote to you offering some arguments against such a proceeding, and am confirmed in the view I took of the subject, by seeing the manner in which the blessed Ferdinand treated some returned emigrants, who went back to their native country on the faith of his promises.[3] I am not a little anxious for your safety during these revolutionary times, and cannot but suppose that Mr Llanos will in some way expose himself to help in the noble cause of regenerating Spain, in such affairs all exertions are dangerous, honour can only be obtained by exposure, and I am the last man to deter the patriot from following the speakings of his conscience. If he desires to be active in the great cause let him be constant and prudent not rash, and foolhardy, his country can be better served by the former, than the latter course—I see that Van Halen [4] has reaped a world of honour in the Belgic revolution, I sincerely congratulate all those in their success who have so nobly shaken off that oppression entailed upon them by the mistakes of ages.—Present my best wishes to Mr Llanos. I am now so chained by business that I cannot hope to visit England for several years, I am the more easy under the confinement since my exertions are crowned with success, giving me a prospect of future wealth and the enjoyment of present comfort and com-

petence. Feeling so easy in my circumstances, I have directed
Reynolds & Simmons not to urge my claim on the Walthamstow
property [5] untill your lein on it is fully liquidated, if when you
are paid there should be a residue, then I shall be well pleased to
receive my claim. Having some expectation that you have removed from your former residence I shall address this to the
care of Reynolds & S. if you are in London M[r] Cuthbertson will
call and tell you how we all are, namely. self Wife, Georgiana,
Emma, Isabel, John, and Clarence.[6] I should be pleased to
hear from you and hope you will not give me cause to complain
of neglect. Having but little time to write many letters I can
only spare time to subscribe myself your very affectionate
Brother

Geo. Keats.

[1] Who had replaced James Rice (died December, 1832). Much later Dilke
gave his name as Arthur Symons.

[2] He also carried a letter of the same date to Dilke (*KC* I, 331f.).

[3] Martin A. S. Hume, *Modern Spain* (New York, 1909), p. 256, remarks:
"Modern civilisation has seen no such instance of brutal, blind ferocity as that
which followed the arrival of Fernando in Madrid," November, 1823.

[4] See p. 55, above, and Part VI, "La revolución de Bruselas en 1830," in Pío
Baroja's *Juan Van Halen* (Madrid, 1933), pp. 303–330.

[5] Which Abbey mortgaged to Llanos: see p. 62, below.

[6] His dates are 1830–1861. After the first two children's names Fanny Llanos
penciled "Emily" and "Frances," and then added after George's signature
"Rosalind, the 2nd, dead I suppose/ See June 5 1825."

-»» 19 «««-

VALENTIN LLANOS TO GEORGE KEATS[1]

3 January 1831 (?)

My dear Sir, What must you think of us and our pro-
tracted silence especially after ⟨the⟩ your letter to M[r] Dilke, in
which you confered upon us ⟨a benefit⟩ an obligation as disinterested as it was timely? [2] Probably, that we are ingrates entirely undeserving of it, ⟨and indeed appearances would justify
your entertaining such thoughts.⟩ nor can I help acknowledging

that you would be borne out by appearances in forming such judgement upon our conduct. Yet I flatter myself you will ⟨come to⟩ arrive at a different conclusion after perusing these few lines. Indeed, were I not conscious of harbouring ⟨unfeigned⟩ in my breast aught but sentiments of the most unfeigned friendship and gratitude, I should not attempt to address you now when every thing conspires to incriminate me in your eyes. On the very day that ⟨we heard from⟩ Mr Dilke ⟨the⟩ communicated to us that part of your letter which concerned us, I ⟨took up my pen⟩ went my course ⟨went⟩ homewards with the intention of writing to thank you for the obligation you had confered upon us, an obligation the more important as it removed difficulties and objections which threatened to involve me and my family in the most serious troubles, and perhaps ruin. You may therefore imagine ⟨that⟩ I was anxious to impart to you the greatful sentiments your brotherly conduct had inspired me with, ⟨were of too greatful a nature not to urge me on to the pleasant task of communicating with one who had from⟩ and that with as little delay as possible; but having ⟨received immediately on the same day your information⟩ on my way home called upon Mr Reynolds, who gave me to understand that the affair of the mortgage ⟨for the conclusion of which I had so much toiled⟩ was to be finally ⟨arranged⟩ settled on the following day, I defered writing ⟨that I might be able to tell you⟩ in order to profit by the opportunity to inform you how matters were arranged. A delay of several days, however, ⟨took place⟩ from the part of Mr Reynolds took place and even ⟨when⟩ after the mortgage was paid off to the amount of £2500 I was left so much in ignorance with respect to the manner in which the remaining £400 were secured that up to this day I ⟨cannot positively say⟩ have not been able to ascertain it, though ⟨of course⟩ you may well imagine I have taken some trouble to find it out. The most painful part, however, of this business, and one indeed which has had no little influence in inducing me to remain silent is what I am about to relate, though I assure you I do it with consider-

able reluctance and regret, ⟨and I would wish⟩ nay, were it not
that I think myself bound to impart to you those circumstances,
I should altogether have suppress[ed] them here. The amount
of the trust funds being ascertained and ⟨agreed to there⟩ in-
vested by the trustees in the Bank of England, there remained a
balance in ⟨my⟩ ⟨our⟩ favour of ⟨about £⟩ Mʳˢ L. and self of
about £780. This sum was handed over to Mʳ Reynolds by the
trustees that it might be paid over to us, and ⟨Mʳ R said that⟩ he
⟨intend⟩ instead of immediately paying ⟨it to us⟩ the whole
balance to us gave us a checque for scarcely half the amount, and
kept ³ back the rest for reasons which he either does not choose
or is unable to explain. A series of disappointments too long to
detail here (but brought on in a great measure by ⟨the⟩ Mʳ R's
neglect of my business) had compelled me to contract debts ⟨the
greatest part of which was paid off by the money I had thus [?]
to⟩ ⟨to a little money⟩ which the sum I then received from Mʳ
R. was scarce sufficient to cover—As far, however, as that sum
went I paid them off; but the consequence was that ⟨instead of
a⟩ I got rid of my ready cash in the vain expectation of being
able ⟨to⟩ with the remainder to ameliorate our circumstances by
applying it to the establishment of a clever and useful patent
invention for which I have paid upwards of £1000, and which I
shall now be obliged to sacrifice for what I may get,⁴ and I find
myself ⟨now⟩ at present in as bad, or rather worse, a predicament
than before. Mʳ R. though well acquainted with our circumstances, and aware of the deep injury he is doing me, by the
delay, not only ⟨does not pay me⟩ continues withholding the
money but has adopted the plan of never being at home to us, or
even vouchsafing an answer to our repeated letters. On the other
hand Mʳ Dilke, to whom I have communicated the facts, de-
clines interfering on the ground that it would involve him in a
quarrel with his friend Rey. forgetting that I have as good a
claim upon the trustees for having paid over the money without
any consent of ours to R. as upon the latter—⟨who⟩ As, however,
I know the ⁵ money has really been paid into R's hands, I have

⟨said nothing⟩ not thought it advisable to tell M⟨r⟩ D. so; ⟨but⟩ and
no alternative is now left me ⟨but to try⟩ to recover it but the
unpleasant one of bringing the matter before a court. That I
have done all I could to avoid this you may ⟨well imagine⟩ infer
from the fact that I have allowed, at the imminent peril of my
personal liberty, upwards of five months to elapse since the ⟨aff⟩
mortgage affair was settled, and ⟨after all⟩ tried all ⟨means⟩ the
arguments ⟨and⟩ & resorted to all the ⟨means within my reach⟩
friendly warnings to bring him to a sense of justice. This explanation will I have no doubt prove to you a satisfactory
apology for my silence; which I ⟨could⟩ felt I could not break
before without being guilty of concealment for I could not
bring up my mind to make accusations of such a nature without ⟨giving⟩ affording the man ⟨as full much⟩ all this time to
clear himself from them. Now, however, that I see the ⟨useless-
ness⟩ fallacy of such expectations, I hasten to write to you, sorry
only that I have no better account to render to you. ⟨Were⟩ To
you this account must be ⟨parti⟩ the more unpleasant as even
your good wishes & kindness toward us have been in some
measure defeated, nor can I help apprehending that in spite
of your declaration to M⟨r⟩ Dilke ⟨of allowing us the precedence
in the mortgage for the amount of money. . .to us⟩ M⟨r⟩ R.
though well acquainted with your intention will when legally
called upon to explain his conduct of waiving your claim in the
morgage until we had received the whole of the money thereby
secured to us, urge in justification the necessity he was under
of retaining the portion belonging to you in the mortgage, and
should M⟨r⟩ D. by a reason similar to that he has already given
me for not interfering in this affair declare showing the letter
you sent him on this subject, the consequences to us may have
the most serious results, though my opinion of M⟨r⟩ D. is that he
would not be guilty of so great an injustice. If, however, ⟨it
seems [?] some⟩ you should hit upon the means to obviate this
⟨should suggest themselves to you⟩ I know you will give us the
benefit of it, and the more readily as it will easily occur to you

that such justification would be only a pretext on the part of
Mʳ R. to retain for himself what he has no earthly right to. In
conclusion I ought to tell you that previous to the settlement of
the mortgage affair, I caused Abbey to execute a bill of Sale for
£300 secured upon his chattels, cattle & on his premises at
Walthamstow, which is also in the hands of Mʳ Reynolds. This
bond is from Abbey to myself; but should it be made available
(of which there is no chance as long as it is in R's hands) and
the goods ⟨there⟩ at Walh. fetch the sum secured by the bond,
there would be about [6] £160 coming to you to which I shall
have to add two years' interest which is now owing from me to
you, and which I intended to have paid with the money obtained
by the mortgage   If I succeeded in ⟨settling this unpleasant
business with Mʳ R.⟩ ⟨obtained my end⟩ recovering the money
from Mʳ R. you may rely on my loosing no time to get it away
from him & inforcing the said bond or try to obtain⟨ing⟩ the
amount of it if possible; for Abbey's situation is now so desperate
that we run a fair chance of losing the benefit of even this
trifling security.[7]

⟨Passing⟩ A few days ago I met Mʳ Wylie, from whom [8] ⟨in-
formed me⟩ I was very sorry to hear that Mʳˢ K. was at the time
you wrote suffering from a most dangerous and alarming illness, but as he had received no further news from you, and the
proverb says that bad news travels fast, I hope she is now perfectly recovered.

*   *   *

[1] A "crossed" draft in which all the canceled words that can be deciphered
are given. The letter actually sent seems to be referred to as dated January 3,
1831, in George's letter of March 24, 1831, following.

[2] On May 7, 1830 (*KC* I, 330), George wrote Dilke that he wished his sister
to "get from it [Abbey's Walthamstow property] *all* her demands upon it, and if
when she has been fully paid there is any left, I shall be well pleased to receive
it."

[3] *Changed from* keeping.

[4] For George's comments to Dilke on the foolish bridle-bits patent of
December 15, 1828, see the letter referred to in note 2.

[5] *Changed from* that.

[6] Athenaeum *is written above* would be about.

[7] For George's comments on the matters Llanos here discusses, see his letter to Dilke of May 11, 1832 (*KC* II, 5). Dilke's reply of February 12, 1833 (*KC* II, 9), shows that Reynolds had a "total incapacity to pay money."

[8] *Originally* who.

→≫ 20 ≪←

GEORGE KEATS TO VALENTIN LLANOS AND
FANNY KEATS DE LLANOS
2 4 March 1 8 3 1

Louisville March 24ᵗʰ 1831.
Mʳ V. Llanos. My dear Sir

Your letter of the 3ʳᵈ Janʸ is now before me.[1] I am sorry Mʳ Reynolds should have caused you so much mortification and distress: it is scarcely possible that he can plead my rights as an excuse for withholding from you your's, since I wrote to Reynolds & Simmons April 22ⁿᵈ 1830 nearly as follows "Is the interest I have in the Walthamstow property worth any thing, calculating that I am not to receive any thing untill Mʳˢ Llanos has recᵈ to the full amount of her mortgage." [2] Again in a letter sent by Mʳ Cuthbertson dated 22ⁿᵈ Nov. 1830 I wrote to them to this amount "I sincerely hope that the Walthamstow property will produce enough to pay Mʳˢ Llanos' *claim,* if after she is fully paid there is a residue I shall be pleased to receive *mine"* Mʳ Cuthbertson wrote on the 1ˢᵗ Febʸ from London stating that R & S said so and so, from which I infer that he has seen them and of course delivered my letter. I cannot therefore but doubt that the 400£ you speak of can be retained by plea of my claims. When I resolved on placing Fanny on the footing I have thought proper to do, I could not do it more effectively than by writing to Reynolds and Dilke; I did not write to you on the subject because I had every reason to beleive that you would leave England for Spain before my letter would reach you, my last letter to you was dated 11 Nov 1829,[3] since which date I have not heard from you; It is therefore your own fault that you have not heard directly from me my intentions relating to this matter. I must confess that I have felt hurt that Fanny has paid so little attention to me as well lately, as when she knew how Abbey was imposing upon me formerly, and how entirely I depended on his integrity, a little information from her on subjects of so much importance to my pecuniary interests was called for by the occasion, and might be considered fairly due from her to me. However well these discrepancies may entitle her to punishment I hope she will escape any serious loss in this present affair. Please to write to me without any delicate reserves if there will be any residue after you are satisfied, and should the money fall into your hands remit it to me without loss of time. It seems to me that in the present disturbed state of Europe in general and of England in particular that there is much danger of the public funds and that the Trustees of Mrs Llanos' estate might safely invest her money in some other way that would produce a better Interest and be more certain. Money is worth here 6 per Cent (legal Interest) and could be loaned on mortgage of real estate valued so low that loss would be almost impossible. M^{rs} K desires her respects. I am

Your Friend & Brother

Geo. Keats.

My dear Fanny.

I must decline sending Tom's miniature [4] in consequence of the great uncertainty of its return and even of its delivery to you if sent, I am not willing to risk the loss of it; if ever I come to England it shall be my companion. Do not expect me before 1836. I hope the annexed note to R & S. will make a desireable settlement with them easy, if Mr Llanos' idea of the cause of his ruggedness is correct you may thank your *neglect* of me for all consequent misfortunes, but for *that* you will have rec^{d} such a note as this earlier in the business. We are all in pretty good health and living very comfortably. Write me something about the estimate which the literati have of John's works, I see Lord Byron has used him vilely in his correspondence,[5] adopting the abominable epithets of the blackguard Blackwood: he pretends all his dislike arose from John's strictures on the Pope school, I think however that Byron took to himself some of the criticism in Sleep and Poetry. How would he like to be estimated by his "hours of Idleness." His praise of Hyperion seems to me totally inconsistent with his more commonly expressed opinions, posterity cannot surely have any thing to do with the Johnny Keats he so often despises and rediculres—Salute my nephew and neice for me and be a better correspondent in future to Your affectionate Brother

Geo. Keats

[1] Probably the letter copied from the preceding draft.
[2] He mentioned this letter to Dilke on May 7, 1830 (*KC* I, 330).
[3] Probably he meant November 15 (see No. 17, above).
[4] She had asked for it in her letter of May 31, 1826 (*KC* I, 299). The miniature is now in the Keats-Shelley House, Rome.
[5] George had been reading Harper's New York edition (2 vols., 1830–31) of Thomas Moore's *Letters and Journals of Lord Byron: with Notices of His Life.*

→》 21 《←

GEORGE KEATS TO JOHN HAMILTON REYNOLDS[1]

6 May 1832

Mr John Reynolds   Louisville Kentucky—May 6th—1832

Copy   Dear Sir,

Having reason to believe that my sister is much in need of money and supposing that you may have some of mine in your hands, I send her annex'd request for £100, or the Balance of acc^t if less than that sum. The Bal^ce of acc^t in my favor sent by M^rs K was £295.6.9. M^rs K rec^d on it £130—I am ignorant of am^t of your charges. In same acc^t you are credited by £100 remitted by Rice to pay Exp's on returned Dft.[2] I will not argue which of us should lose this sum, but retain you as my Councillor to suggest the pros against your own cons, and however much the pros may beat the cons in argument, I am willing to compromise with a credit to me of £50. It is not impossible that something may be realised out of the Walthamstow Mortgage by the arrival of this. I most ardently hope you will feel justified in paying the order. Altho' I am in very thriving circumstances, a heavy money pressure now operating here, renders the abstraction of ever so small a sum from my business, an injury to my partner as well as myself; £100 is a much more important sum here, than it is with you—present my respects to your Father & Mother, and kind remembrances to Sisters, I hope in 1836 to shake hands with your facetious Brother,[3] whose every annual is in my Bookcase, in company with the works he presented to me, I will thank him in person some day for the present, and the pleasure I have derived from the contents. Tell Mr Dilke he will hear from me soon. I hope Mr Rice enjoys better health than formerly. truly your's sig^d / Geo. Keats.

Copy of order refer'd to.

£100.———$\frac{00}{100}$ Louisville May 6th 1832

At sight please to pay to the order of Mrs Llanos One Hundred pounds Sterling or the Balance in my favor in your hands if less than that amount, and much oblige   Sig^d/Geo. Keats.
To Jno H Reynolds
      London.

[1] A copy in an unidentified hand. The original was presumably not mailed until May 12 (see the postmark of the next letter).

[2] On this unaccepted draft see p. 40, above.

[3] Thomas Hood, who married Jane Reynolds in 1825. His *Comic Annual* ran to eleven volumes, 1830–39, 1842. Hood may have known George, but (as Professor Alvin Whitley tells me) in an unpublished letter of October 8, 1844, to one Watson he says of John Keats. "I did not know him personally."

->>> 22 <<<-

GEORGE KEATS TO FANNY KEATS DE LLANOS

6 (?) May 1832

Address: Mrs Llanos./ care of Henry Shea Esqre/ N° 10. Dowgate Hill.¹/
Mansion House/ London/ England.
Postmarks: LOUISVILLE KY MAY 12; PAID; LIVERPOOL SH{IP
LETTER}; G 20 JU 20 1832

My dear Sister. Cut off the above and present it to Mr Reynolds
for payment,² I hope and trust it will produce to you the am^t
it calls for. Your letters of 25 Jany and 18 Feby were a long
time on the way, the latter came first to hand and the former
was waited for to explain ⟨the latter⟩ its meaning. Having had
such bad fortune in my English concerns, some of which I
beleive you are unacquainted with, I have given up all attention
to them untill I can arrange them in person some years hence
perhaps in 1836. You have doubtless heard an exaggerated
picture of my wealth, from what quarter I know not, it is as well
however to apprize you of the real facts. I am engaged with one
partner ³ in a very extensive, and sufficiently profitable business,
that requires a very large capital, and shall if no great commercial distress takes place be wealthy in a few years. Untill
1828 I was struggling with difficulties, that seemed from time to
time insurmountable, and sufficient to have broken the spirit
of many men, I had previous to that time prospects, and hopes,
that a sanguine temperament will always suggest, in that year
however I reallized three times my expences including Mrs Keats
visit to England; since then I have regularly added to my
capital, and real estate, partly by business, and partly by
judicious purchases of property. I intend to continue in my
present timber business untill I have built houses enough to
yeild an annual rent sufficient to support my family in a liberal
manner; when if the acquisitiveness of my character does not
"encrease by what it feeds on" ⁴ I shall retire from my present

engrossing occupation, and visit the country of my youth. Upon my real estate rests my credit, which has hitherto enabled me to extend my business to any extent, by paying an Interest of about 6¾ per Cent, within these 3 months however the U. S. Bank has been withdrawing its loans, thereby reducing my business capital, and the circulating medium generally, making the collection of debts more difficult than heretofore, and causing me considerable trouble, and a general stagnation. Under these circumstances it will require all my means and management to swim where so many are sinking. Before the pressure began, our house had commenced two extensive buildings, a Saw Mill cost 10,000 dollars, a planing Mill and patent right 8,000 dollars, both of which are now in operation, and requiring more capital to carry them on, than we have hitherto required—Being the man of business of the concern, my partner being principally engaged in the Yards, and attending to the superintendence of the hands, nearly all responsibility rests with me. It is true we have as much owing to us as we need, owing however to the s[c]arcity of money we cannot collect our funds, and are therefore hard pressed to carry on with our accustomed punctuallity our extended concerns. I give you this outline to show you, that altho' I am thriving and shall probably become wealthy, I am not now so rich as you seem to think. I am obliged to you for your congratulations on my prosperity, which considering the circumstances that have surrounded me is truly astonishing to myself when I look back to the past. What is termed rich here, is very moderate independence in England—£1000 a year from real estate is Called rich, my expences are about 600£ a year and I live handsomely without paying much attention to minute economy. At the time I invited you to come to Kentucky I did it in sincerity of heart and with a hope of seeing you—I did not urge you warmly because I doubted if you would be pleased with the society of the place, or our mode of living which at that time was very quiet, and because it might seem that I had interested motives for so doing. You were at the time in good circumstances as I thought, and no destitute orphan, certainly better off than I was, and without encumbrances, I did not look upon you as uncherished or unprotected or in any respect in want of a home. Your letter of complaint contained the intention you had of "changing your condition," [5] which I asked you to explain, and which meant that you were going to be married, I presume then that your marriage, and not the coldness of my invitation must have determined you not to come to America. If you were better acquainted with my disposition you would not have thought for an instant that my invitation was a mere form, "a sugar plumb." M^rs K and myself often talked about providing for your comfort and amusement. As to my neglecting to arrange to bring you out, what steps could I have taken beyond assisting you after your arrival at New York, which I promised to do. Your pathetic description of my indifference and unfeeling conduct towards you, is, I can assure you a mere "man of Straw," and only requires a candid and unprejudiced reperusal of my letters to overturn it. I remember distinctly that I always invited a regular correspondence, and was seldom indulged with a letter. No more of this, let it be forgotten, it shall never be again revived by me.—My hands are so full that I have neither time nor capital to apply to any new concern, and if I had both I have obtained enough experience, to be sure, that money cannot be made in any business that is not well understood by those who carry it on. Your project might possibly succeed in one of [the] Eastern cities, in the hands of a man who perfectly understands it, and is withal a man of business, but here I am sure however feasible and economical the plan may be, it would not succeed. You may suppose how unprepared we {are} for works of the kind you mention, when you hear that our Streets are not lighted at all, and we are not yet furnished with water works: there are not any Gas works West of the Alleganies. I hope soon to hear from Mr Llanos agreeably to his promise, and sincerely wish that his future undertakings will result more prosperously than the past. I regret much to learn that he has so much cause of dissatisfaction with Reynolds, who seems to have behaved in a most unaccountable manner. My best resp^ts and wishes to Mr L. and love to the children and rem^s to the Wylie's. I am

Your affectionate Brother
Geo. Keats.

On reflection I hardly think it probable that this will find you in London, it cannot arrive untill the end of June and you propose starting for Spain in the Spring. M^rs K had purchased some presents to be sent to England by a Friend who will probably arrive in Liverpool in August, and under the impression that you will have departed before that time she has returned the one intended for you.

¹ Shea is listed as a merchant at this address in Pigot's London directory for 1823–24.

² She cut off about two-thirds of the first page, which presumably bore the original letter of which that preceding (dated May 6) is a copy.

³ Daniel Smith, who lived between Green and Walnut streets on Fifth.

⁴ Compare *Hamlet*, I. ii. 144f.

⁵ See p 20, above. George told Dilke about these complaints on May 11, 1832 (*KC* II, 4f.).

⇢⟫ 23 ⟪⇠

FANNY KEATS DE LLANOS (?) TO GEORGE KEATS[1]

May (?) 1832

My dear brother. About four months ago I wrote to you, informing you of ⟨my⟩ our intended journey to Spain, and explaining ⟨to you⟩ certain circumstances that ⟨had⟩ obliged me to have recourse to you for the loan of £100. Two or three weeks after, I wrote again, to communicate to you a project which I thought might be of service to you, if it could be brought to bear in America. ⟨and⟩ In this letter I also alluded to the subject of our intended visit to Spain, and to the request I had made in my former—I have received no answer To ⟨n⟩either of these letters ⟨I have received no answer⟩, though more than sufficient time has now elapsed for me to have received a reply ⟨to⟩ even to the last. If ⟨I know anything of your character⟩ my estimate of your character be correct, I can not attribute your silence to the request I was compelled by circumstances to make, and am therefore ⟨am quite⟩ the more at a loss to account for it, as I there ⟨urged⟩ begged you would answer me without any delay, that the object ⟨for such⟩ I had in view by making such an application might not be defeated. As matters have turned out the delay has caused me no inconvenience, but it has vexed me, for in spite of the high opinion I have of your character, & the credit I give you for brotherly kindness & generous feelings, ⟨suspicions would intrude that the request I made might have some thing to do with your silence⟩ I cannot help feeling that you are not quite so keenly alive to my comfort and happiness as I had foolishly imagined. I know that I have also sins of omission to answer for to you. ⟨but [?] and therefore little to complain of⟩ Still, I believe, that you would not tak⟨ing⟩e the opportunity of showing me your displeasure ⟨when pressed⟩ at the very time when I apply to you for assistance. Whatever be the cause, I, however, hope that the present may not share the same fate as my former ones. I now write to inform you that owing in some measure to the serious illness of Irene, our eldest child,[2] ⟨our departure may⟩ ⟨in part, and⟩ but principally to the ⟨unfair & unworthy⟩ disgraceful conduct of John Reynolds, who, after retaining a ⟨considerable balance as his, which he had received⟩ sum of money of consequence to us in our present circumstances, to meet, as he says, his account, will neither deliver this nor the money, we have been obliged to suspend our journey,[3] till we see the end of this matter, which we have been obliged to put into the hands of a lawyer, with whom ⟨he⟩ R has been playing the game of a litigious & dishonourable man. ⟨it so happening that neither ⟨either⟩ Mʳ Dilke or Mʳ Rice⟩ This matter might have been greatly simplified had either of the trustees stepped forward in the business; but as ⟨the latter⟩ Mʳ Rice

is the particular friend of R. & ⟨the former⟩ Mr Dilke ⟨does⟩
⟨will⟩ does not ⟨move without the⟩ like to offend either the one
or [4] the other by ⟨pressing⟩ espousing our cause, it must go before a Court if

*   *   *

[1] Since Fanny Llanos wrote to her brother "four months ago" and "two or
three weeks after," that is (see George's letter of May 6 [?], 1832) on January
25 and February 18, this draft in the hand of Llanos but intended, I think, for
his wife was probably written late in May or early in June. Because the Llanoses
postponed their migration to Spain until the following summer, and because
George's letter of May 6 (?) reached London on June 20, one can only hope
that the draft was discarded and not sent.

[2] Who died in January, 1833.

[3] According to Adami, pp. 136f., they went to Spain in the early summer of
1833.

[4] *Written* of.

→⟩⟩ 24 ⟨⟨←

GEORGE KEATS: TWO POEMS[1]

The Influence of tea upon the *Ladies*

Dear Tea, that enlivener of Wit and of Soul,
More loquacious by far than the draughts of the Bowl
Soon unloosens the tongue, and enlivens the mind,
And enlivens the eyes to the faults of mankind,
It brings on the tapis their neighbours defects,
The faults of their Friends, or their wilful neglects,
Reminds them of many a good-natured [2] tale,
About those who are stylish, or those who are frail;
In harmless Chit Chat an acquaintance they roast,
And serve up a friend, as they serve up a toast,
The Wives of our men of inferior degree,
Will sip up repute in a little *Bohea*,
2 { With *Hyson* a beverage still more refin'd,
  { Our Ladies of fashion enliven their mind.

1 { But the scandal improves (a refinement in wrong)
     As our Matrons are richer and rise to *Souchong*,[3]
   And by nods inuendoes and hints and what not
   Reputation and Tea send together to Pot,
   While Madam in Cambrics, & Laces array'd
   With her plate and her liveries in splendid parade,
   Will drink in *Imperial* a friend at a sup,
   Or in *gunpowder,* blow them by dozens all up.

G K

On Woman

Happy a man may pass his life,
If freed from matrimonial chains,
If he's directed by a Wife,
He's sure to suffer for his pains.

What tongue is able to unfold
The falsehoods that in Women dwell,
Virtues in Women you behold,
Are almost imperceptible.

Adam could find no solid peace,
   When Eve was given for a mate
Till he beheld a Woman's face,
   Adam was in a happy state.

For in this sex you'll see appear
   Hypocrisy, deceit, and pride,
Truth, darling of a heart sincere
   In Women never can reside.[4]

Distraction take the men, I say,
   Who make the Women their delight,
Who no regard to Women pay;
   Keep reason always in their sight.

Ceux qui sont plus favorablement enclin vers les dames, qu'ills lisent la première & troisiéme line & ensuite la seconde & quatrième de chaque Vers.

G. K.

[1] Each undated poem is on one side of a single leaf. In the right-hand margin of page 2, penciled and partly erased, is written: "I think George Keats must be a perfect divine if he made these Lines for I am sure he meant to have the first and second line read so—as nothing could proceed from his angelic lips not bearable with respect to the fair sex.

"Signed {Valentin} Llanos"

[2] *Written* good-naturned.

[3] Apparently George intended the couplets to be transposed.

[4] *In the right margin is the word* happy.

→≫ 25 ≪←

JOSEPH SEVERN TO FANNY KEATS DE LLANOS

3 July 1861 [1]

Envelop addressed: Madam Keats Llanos/ with 3 Vols, Rome

B. Consulate July 3

My dear Madam Llanos

At a quarter to 5. today M[r] Odo Russell [2] calls for me to see the Luca della Robbia   If you like at that hour to join us here, with your charming family I shall be glad—

The 3 vols of Rome [3] I now send & beg to say it will be a pleasure to me if you will command me in any thing else for I feel great regret at the loss of your dear society even for awhile & therefore 'tis a pleasure to me that you should possess my books meanwhile, even to remind you of our singular meeting & spontaneous friendship which has been one of those rare things occuring once only in our lives.

I scarce remember if I mentiond to M[r] Brockman [4] the desire I feel to recommend to his notice Sig[e] Francesco Franz the young engineer whom I was so fortunate as to rescue from such a cruel fate [5]—If I did not mention him & my hope that should

a vacancy occur Mr Brockman may kindly employ him; I beg
the favor of you to do so—for I am fully assured of the admirable
character & skill of my protoge—he is 22 years of age

Very Sincerely Yours

Joseph Severn

To Mrs Llanos

[1] Severn was appointed British consul to Rome in January, 1861. Fanny Llanos
with various members of her family arrived there in March. She and Severn met,
appropriately enough, on April 6 in the house wherein Keats had died, and
became at once devoted friends. In July, as the first five letters of the present
series (Nos. 25–29) show, the Llanoses and Brockmanns moved to Naples, where
they remained for over a year.

[2] Odo William Leopold Russell (1829–1884), son of the ninth Duke of Bedford;
attaché at Naples, 1860; on special diplomatic service at Rome, 1860–1870;
created Baron Ampthill of Ampthill, 1881.

[3] Possibly some edition of Paul Letarouilly's *Edifices de Rome moderne* with
three volumes of some three hundred fifty plates.

[4] Leopold Brockmann, husband of Fanny Llanos' daughter Isabel, chief con-
sulting engineer (1861–1864) for the Roman railways that were just being built.
Before leaving Italy he was made a papal count.

[5] Severn "was able to rescue his secretary's brother from prison in Rome by
clever handling of the Papal authorities, and got him a position on the Naples
railways through his influence with the Government of Italy" (Birkenhead,
p. 215). But see Severn's letters of September 21, below.

→≫ 26 ≪←

JOSEPH SEVERN TO FANNY KEATS DE LLANOS[1]

2 1 September 1 8 6 1

Envelop addressed: To/ Madam Keats de Llanos/ Palazzo Serrecapriola/
Chiaja [2]/ Napoli/ per presentare Sig^e F. R. Franz

B. Consulate Sepr 21

My dear Madam Llanos

This is to introduce to your kind notice Sig^r Franceso
Rossler Franz[3] the brother of my Secretary for whom you have
been so much interested on my account

Whilst I am writing this I dont know if he may be able to get

away from Rome, for his Passport was this morning refused &
on my interference I could well understand that some other
persecution was intended, so I insisted on having the Passport
& with much difficulty it was granted, but only on the condition
that he should never return unless with the permission of the
Roman government—

It must be private malice & envy as he was so successfull in
his mathematical studies in the Roman University

I am sure I need not say more to command your kind attention to him

beleive Sincerly Yours
Joseph Severn .

¹ Enclosed in the letter next following (which was written first).
² The Strada di Chiaja.
³ See pp. 74f., above, and p. 77 n., below.

⇢⟫ 27 ⟪←

JOSEPH SEVERN TO FANNY KEATS DE LLANOS¹
21 September 1861

British Consulate Sep 21, 1861

My dear Madam Llanos

How much I regret that I cannot join you at Naples now
that the cool weather has come—It would be such a pleasure to
me to go & see the sights of Naples with you & your charming
family, but I fear that the passing events are so important that
I dare not be away & indeed the stirring events which have trans-
pired since you left Rome, in addition to the great loss of your
society, make it appear like years to me

I am very gratefull to you ² for your kindness in procuring
from Signor Leopoldo ³ the place as Sub engineer under Sigᵉ
Rossi, & which I am sure he would [have accepted] but I have
been astonishd at just hearing that the Roman Police now
refuse his Passport—at the moment I am writing this I dont

know how it will finish, but I have to settle it by a sturdy visit to the Governor of Rome when I have written this—The persecution of this young man is beyond the usual doings here

I am sorry to find that the heat has been so great at Naples as to prevent you going about.—We have kept quietly at home & not sufferd I have been able to paint every day & have begun early in the mor^g,—perhaps my house is remarkably cool & *cold* in the winter.—I am going in a week to the Poli Palace over the Fountain of Trevi where I have an unfurnishd apartment with high windows

It interests me to hear that you are to make such a long sojourn at Naples & I have no doubt that at last I shall find you there before you find me here, for the rail way may be finishd before you leave Naples & then I must go in it in the general rejoicings

As yet I have not got my family nor indeed the news that they have actually set out, so my feares for my dear wifes health are renew'd—My Son [4] is very well, he has always been painting & begs now to be most kindly rememberd to you

You will be very anxious about the well being of Madam Brockman [5] & tis fortunate you went to Naples

Ask Mr Llanos if the Spanish Guittar player went to England after all?

Your Son I am sure must have made a picture of great beauty from the Correggio, judging from his work done at the Doria [6]— Your other son [7] I hope will be soon with you & I conclude will come with his father, then you will be quite happy—Your bird & your humble servant are in the same condition without our coats—his is moulting & mine has been stolen.—he dont yet sing

Good bye, with my love to all your dear ones beleive me Yours sincerely

Joseph Severn

[1] Enclosed with the preceding letter of introduction.

[2] *Written* your.

[3] Brockmann. Severn apparently wrote *Sognior,* and forgot to name the F. R. Franz of the preceding letter.

⁴ Arthur (see p. 92 n., below).

⁵ Leopold's mother.

⁶ Juan ("John" or "my brother brush," as Severn later calls him) copied at the Doria-Pamphili Palazzo, Rome, with its eight hundred pictures.

⁷ Luis (born 1843).

->>> 28 <<<-

JOSEPH SEVERN TO FANNY KEATS DE LLANOS

5 November 1861

Palazzo Poli Tues Novr 5th ¹

My dear Mrs Llanos

I have just got yours of the 1st touching the extraordinary report of Mr Kenrick—'Tis true that he & the Lady were 10 months at the Hotel del'Europa without paying & that Madam Melga the mistress (English) paid their journey to Naples

Also that I strove to get him a situation influenced by the good opinion of Madam Melga (who had certainly paid for it) & also that he wrote me a gentlemanlike letter which satisfied me as regards his education, but I wondered as you do that being pennyless they should think of going to an expensive Hotel so judging from your letter I begin to think them adventurers for what reason but a dishonest one could they have for going to the Vittoria? ²—

I did not apply to Mr Brockman but only to the V. Consul at Chiveti-Vecchia ³ & certainly I have not authorised them to go to you or Mr Bonham—Madam Melga was satisfied of their respectability 'tho she has given up all hope of her money for the relations would have nothing more to do with them

I regret that you should have bestowd [?] any on I fear undeserving people, but yet 'tis my duty to tell you that Madam Melga wishes me to say every thing I can in their favor which I have & which is very little

I thought Miss Brockman looking so well & so handsome & I

trust you all look as well & how I long to see all those looks—
Mr Brockman was also in excellent looks & he gave such a good
account of my protégé Francesco Franz [4] that I was much gratified

My Quadraccio I am glad to tell you is generally admired &
thought to be an original—I am glad that John [5] liked it—You
are right he should [make] some good copies at Naples which
are sure to sell

My dear wife is not yet come & I [am] alarmd lest she is too
ill to come on [6]

Mr Russell has just arrived & brought news that there is *no
chance* of the French *ever* leaving Rome [7]

My new house pleases me much as it is so ample but I shall be
years furnishing it at a pins head a quarter.—

My doings in Rome would astonish you if you could know
them.—I am so rejoiced to hear all the favorable news of your
Naples sojourn & the good resulting from it, My love to all your
dear family & also my Sons who feels with me the length of your
absence   Yours affectionately [8]

Joseph Severn

[1] Tuesday, November 5, came in 1861.

[2] I know nothing about the persons Severn discusses except for E. W. Bonham,
C.B., British consul-general at Naples, Palazzo Calabritto, Strada di Chiaja.
John Murray's *Handbook for Travellers in Southern Italy* (1853) says (pp. 84f.)
that the Gran Bretagna, kept "by S. Melga, brother of the landlord of the
Europa [in the Piazza di Spagna] at Rome, and formerly master of the Crocelle,
is now, perhaps, the best hotel in Naples," but that the Vittoria, on the Largo
della Vittoria is "not inferior, except in situation." Murray's 1858 edition
remarks (p. 64) that the charges at the Vittoria "have been complained of lately."

[3] *So apparently for* Civita Vecchia.

[4] See pp. 74–76, above.

[5] For John see p. 78 n., above. Severn intended to write *quadruccio*, a small
picture.

[6] She died at Marseilles in April, 1862.

[7] Russell (see p. 75 n., above) was a poor prophet, for they left in 1870.

[8] The word looks like "affectiontivly."

→» 29 «←

JOSEPH SEVERN TO FANNY KEATS DE LLANOS
22 August 1862

Envelop addressed: To/ Madam Keats de Llanos/ Castleamare/ J.
Severn favored by Henry Wreford Esq[r] [1]/ Palazzo Illino

Rome Pal. Poli Aug 22

My dear M[rs] Llanos

As I wrote you almost two months ago, & fear you never
got my letter, I take the opportunity of a friend going to Naples
M[r] Wreford to trust this to his carefull hand

I had the pleasure to hear of your well being from Lady C.
Stuart [2] to whom you had been so kind that she spoke of it
several times very gratefully & gave me your kind request that
I would visit you at Castleamare [3]   this would indeed be a
gratification to me but I fear 'tis impossible for in addition to
the very important things occurring daily & in which I am of
use inasmuch as I can do good to suffering people & also the
momentious nature of Rome itself; I have now my "Marriage
of Cana" [4] which begins to be a kind of daily inchantment to
me, as it is the best composition I have ever made—there are 26
figures & I am just commencing to paint them from nature my
picture being all painted in with transparent colours So you
will perceive that however I might find Rome dull, this picture
serves to enliven my solitude

I have the pleasure to hear that M[r] Brockman is just now
returning & trust to have the gratification of seeing him—

I think you know that my Son Arthur went to London last
month & is now in full activity with his brot[r] doing the illu-
minated almanack, with M[rs] Norton writing the poetry—[5]

I have invited my eldest daughter M[rs] Gale [6] to spend the
winter with me as I am concernd to find that she has been
suffering from a cough all the time of my Consulate, I dont

know if she will come as she has a very young family—I hope
your dear baby [7] is well & growing beautifully as he was in Rome
& also that his charming mama lets him cry that he may have a
fine voice Then I can fancy I hear Rosa's [8] piano for she
fascinated the Countess [9] with her music & I trust that the Miss
Brockmans are well thro' this intense heat & in good health—
It has even beat our famous Tivoli—Then I trust your own
dear self is in full enjoyment of health in your beautifull sojourn

M[r] Wreford who kindly takes this is the admirable "Times
correspondent" & is now on his way to Sicily—He is sadly disappointed that the railway is not open as he lookd forward to
going to & fro continually from Rome to Naples [10]—If M[r] Brockman could permit him to go when there is the chance of a train
it would be a very great favour, indeed I think he might be of
service in making known in England the *cruel position of the
railway*—of which I hear *no hopes* of opening—I shall be very
glad to hear from you & beg to present my love to all your dear
circle—Did M[r] Llanos go to London? & is John [11] painting?

Yours very sincerely

Joseph Severn

[1] Wreford was the author of *Le Prigioni italiane dinanzi al governo ed al
parlamento. Lettere tre del Cav. Enrico Wreford corrispondente del Thimes*
(Naples, 1869). Another hand added "Palazzo Illino" on the envelop, which,
like the letter paper, is black-edged (Severn's wife had died in April).

[2] Emmeline Bathurst, wife of the third Earl of Castle Stewart (1807–1857), who
at the Villa Stuart, Rome, June 27, 1867, married Alessandro Pistocchi, chevalier
of the Legion of Honor, and died there on January 7, 1893. Her father was
Benjamin Bathurst, the diplomat (1784–1809) whose death in Germany remains
one of the great unsolved mysteries of the century.

[3] Castellammare di Stabia on the Bay of Naples.

[4] See pp. 82, 87, 89, 94, 99, below.

[5] *The Golden Calendar. With a Perpetual Almanac Illustrated by Walter
Severn. And with New Poems by Various Authors* (London, n.d. [1865]). Dedi-
cated to the Princess Mary of Cambridge, the book contains verses by some twenty-
five poets, but no Norton is anywhere mentioned.

[6] Claudia Fitzroy Severn married Frederick Gale (1823–1904), barrister and
well-known cricket player, in 1852. She died in 1874.

[7] Isabel Brockmann's son Ernesto.

[8] Fanny Llanos' fourth child (1832–1905).

[9] Lady Castle Stewart (see note 2).

[10] The Caserta and Capua line, connecting Naples with Rome, was begun in December, 1843, but was not completed till the end of August, 1862. Three other lines of 719 miles were under contract to the Bastoggi Company, which engaged to complete them in 1868.

[11] Juan Llanos (1831–1905).

-->> 30 <<--

JOSEPH SEVERN TO FANNY KEATS DE LLANOS
9 February, March 1867[1]

Rome Feb 9th 1867

My dear Friends

You wrote me a most beautifull letter of condolence which I often read & which amongst the many I received is to me the most true & consoling, but I have never quite recovered [from] the [2] blow & I fear I never shall—but I'll try to be cheerfull & not write sadness of which you have already too much

You kindly ask about my painting & of this I can answer favorably—my picture of the marriage at Cana is now very near done [3] & all my f[ds] think it the best of all my works, for I have [been] able to indulge myself in taking all means to make it perfect—the subject is so beautifull & also my view of it is quite my own [4] so these were great inducements   I should have sent it to the Paris exhibition

March 22

but for serious illness during the whole winter not only two attacks of Bronchitis (not so bad as when I first had the happiness to meet you) also a general rheumatism particularly in my right arm and this prevented me finishing my picture & still makes me feel 90 years old!

My daughter Eleanor is in England where she went Dec[r] 9th to attend Walters marriage with Mary Dalrymple Fergusson [5] & where she is to remain until October, for last summer she had a nervous fever & I had great fears of losing her, but fortunately

I had that beautifull Villa at Frascati belonging to the King of
Italy (which His Majesty lends me most graciously eve[r]y
year) & that set her up for she was enchanted—she had the company of Miss Winter [6] who has been staying with us ever since
you left Rome—Left Rome! what a loss to me & I now feel it
more than ever as I am alone for we lived in charming friendship as tho' we had always lived together & as tho' it was to
last for ever.—Yet as I well remember you had a serious objec-
tion to my ugly gigantic staircase; you will now be pleased to
hear, that I am to have the Florence Palace which by the treaty
of Peace has become the property of the Italian crown & which
consigns to me as His representive & also for the services which
I have rendered to the Italian gov[t], but I dont know when I am
to get possession for the Papal party is so openly indignant that
they declare they'l rather burn down the Palace than that I
should live in it,—& as the plan of the Italian gov[t] is now to
conciliate the priesthood at *any price,* so I must bide my time,
but I cannot help telling you that there is a good staircase & so
there may be a chance in these wonderfull times of your coming
to keep house with me in this Ambassadorial Palace, which retains its fine furniture & has a garden! & I shall thus be rent
free [7]—Is there a chance of your ever coming to Rome again?
The project of the Marcian Acqueduct which I remember was
just talked of when you left is now well set up in an Anglo
Roman comp[y] & the work going on but without the old acqueduct!! [8] It was found easier & cheaper to convey the water by
cast iron pipes straight to Rome, the affair has been warmly
taken up & directed by M[r] Shepherd of the Gas—I have taken 50
Shares at £20 each & all the shares were sold in a week! for the
Rome caught at them with the greatest avidity [9]—As I bore in
mind what you intimated that dear Count Brockman would
undertake such a work so I proposed him to M[r] Shepherd, but
the change of plan to the iron pipes had obliged him to find an
engineer connected with the iron works—he is a frenchman—
but the work does not make much progress as yet Lady Castle

Stuart [10] was just now here & begs me to remember her most kindly to you all—Now how I should like to know that dear Brockman is well establishd in health & satisfied with his present occupation of banker,[11] that the charming Countess & her dear ones are well & that Rosa [is] still filling the house with her divine harmonies   she still retains her place as the *pearl* of my picture [12]—

You see I am going to indulge in another halfsheet—I am afraid you will not be able to write me about many pleasant *present* things but that we shall be obliged to go back & back for our enjoyment with the pen—I am sorry to tell you that I made nothing of Ld Houghton, who even snubbed me as regards my notes to "Adonais" [13]   my son thought he was jealous of any compe[ti]tion as he was bringing out a larger edition of his life of your illustrious brother [14] & he never answered me about yourself & the pension—[15]

Here in Rome none of my countrymen think (not even Mr Gladstone [16]) that there is any need of a new tomb   on the contrary they all prefer to see the old one—the Box you planted [17] has grown up full 3 feet & is very solid & ample for the lovers of the Poet

You kindly enquire after my Son Arthur who I am glad to say is a model goo[d] boy—He continues to advance in his painting, & sell his works & I continually hear great praises even from Strangers who enquire if I am related to him! You pleasantly tell me that you are all united in one house & that you are opposite the Gallery of pictures & you very kindly invite me to pay you a long visit which would indeed be charming, but I am here tied by the leg for life perhaps & indeed I doubt that the F. O. would let me leave even for a day!

March 30 I am glad to tell you that I am now getting better & can write with comparitive ease   You must tell me how my brother brush is getting on   do send me one of Louis's Caricatures—I congratulate you on having another grandson & I have no doubt he is as handsome as the first

I am greatly amused on having to think *only of myself now* for all my life I have been doing & thinking for others, now I study egotism in every shape & enjoy all its oddities *for me* [18]

Good bye my dear friends & pardon the delay which my illness has caused

Yours very sincerely

Joseph Severn

[1] Severn's dates of March 22, 30 are wrong, for the letter is accompanied by an envelop addressed "a/ Madam Keats di Llanos/ Calle de Lope de Vega No 61—Cuarto derecha/ piso 2do/ Madrid/ J. S." (actually Severn is writing to the whole family), with various postmarks, as Rome on March 23, Lyons and Marseilles on March 26, Madrid on March 29, while at the top of what he calls "another halfsheet" Fanny Llanos penciled "Mar 20 1867."

[2] *Written* the the. Severn's artist-daughter, Ann Mary, who had married the archaeologist Charles Thomas Newton (1816–1894) on April 27, 1861, died in London on January 2, 1866.

[3] See p. 99, below.

[4] Eric Robertston (in Sharp, p. 303) says that the picture "evinced a touch of genius in representing the transformed water poured from one pitcher at first transparent as crystal, but changing colour in its arc, like a rainbow, and descending red into the other pitcher."

[5] Daughter of Sir Charles Dalrymple Fergusson, Bart. She and Walter Severn (October 12, 1830–September 22, 1904) married on December 28, 1866.

[6] Birkenhead, pp. 222f., says that Victor Emmanuel gave Severn, who in 1864 was made consul at Rome for the kingdom of Italy, his royal Frascati villa for the summers of 1864 and 1865. Evidently Severn also had it in 1866 and was expecting it in 1867. It is at least possible that Miss Winter is the person mentioned by Keats in *Letters*, p. 309.

[7] The Palazzo di Firenze, near the Palazzo Borghese, was in 1867 the property of the Tuscan government and the residence of its minister to the Vatican. Severn did not get it but remained to the end in the Palazzo Poli.

[8] The Aqua Marcia was first brought to Rome in 145 B.C. The project Severn speaks of, involving restoration as well as the use of some sixteen miles of iron pipes, was completed in September, 1870.

[9] See pp. 87, 89, 98, below. *Severn intended to write* for the Romans.

[10] See p. 80, above.

[11] A fact not noted by Adami, pp. 175f. See p. 89, below.

[12] Sharp, p. 251 n., and Adami, p. 158, say that Isabel Brockmann was one of the models for "The Marriage of Cana." Severn's comment here and on p. 99, below, about Rosa Llanos indicates that they were mistaken.

[13] For years Severn hoped to publish "a folio edition of the 'Adonais,' with annotations and notes, to be illustrated after specially made designs by himself

and his two artist-sons, Walter and Arthur" (Sharp, p. 213; see also p. 257, and Birkenhead, p. 233).

[14] *The Life and Letters of John Keats . . . A New Edition* (London, 1867).

[15] Severn wrote to Houghton on September 28, 1864 (*KC* II, 326f.), suggesting that he approach Lord Palmerston about granting Mme. Llanos a pension.

[16] Gladstone as a member of Lord Russell's government had appointed Severn consul to Rome. Fanny Llanos and Severn had planned in 1864 to erect a new tombstone over Keats's grave (Adami, pp. 163–165).

[17] Sharp, p. 252 n., and Adami, p. 161, say that she planted two bay trees beside her brother's grave.

[18] See his restatement on pp. 89, 95, below.

->>> 31 <<<-

JOSEPH SEVERN TO FANNY KEATS DE LLANOS

2 9 March 1 8 6 9

Envelop addressed: To/ M^rs di Llanos/ Calle de Lope de Vega N° 61/ Cuarto derecha piso 2do/ Madrid/ J. S. Rome
Postmarks (some imperfect): ROMA 5 APR 69; 3 F AVRIL 69 3 St MICHEL; PP; PARIS ETRANGER 69 8 AVRIL; BORDEAUX A 9 AVRIL 69; MADRID (1) 10 ABR 69

BRITISH CONSULATE. ROME [1]

29th March 1869

My dear Mrs de Llanos

The great pleasure of seeing dear Lewis has resolved the mystery of my never hearing from you—two letters of mine & one of Eleanors have remained what? in the post,—never deliverd? or how

We are inchanted to hear good news of you all & with it to call up your charming sojourn in Rome & a vivid remembrance of those happy days from the day when you & I met like brother & sister, when we sat in silence hand in hand with your daughters, mutually astonishd at such a meeting & in such a place—twas a romance *aye & is so still*

you will no doubt have heard of Lord Houghton having

publishd a new edition of your illustrious brothers life with many additions, also a 2ᵈ Vol of all the Poems which I have not yet got, the life is very beautifully printed ²

I have got my dear twins with me at present—they have grown strong & really clever—Eleanor still improves in the "gift of the gab" & has been acting with great success—Arthur is doing the artist in good style & even making money, his drawings I see now for the first time tho' many strangers ask me if the young artist is related to me!!

I have been a sufferer from rheumatism & am still, tho much less & last Autumn I was struck down by inflamations of the bowels, which nearly did for me, indeed my Roman fᵈˢ say that I ought to have died for that they alway die!! eating an excess of fruit the cause

Rome is much as you left it except that the acqua Marcia which was just commenced is now near completion & bids fair to be a fine & usefull undertaking   I have 50 Shares in it & have paid a thousand pounds ³—It is to supply a very fine water up to the top stories as it comes from a lake up in the mountains 38 miles of between Tivoli & Subiaco

Will you ever visit Rome again? I am afraid not for now that you are all settled at Home with all your interests to cultivate, twill be difficult to move about

Here am I going on just as you left me with no change but my hair tumbling of—My Sectⁱᵉˢ ⁴ the same, but my house is very much brushd up & I have the meetings of the English Archaeological Society ⁵—my painting flourishes tho the marriage at Cana is not quite done but I have taken great pains with it ⁶

Lewis has grown such a fine lad & I was delighted to find that he has such a charming appointment

Dear Rosa excells in her beautifull Music as much as ever, & the Count & Countess with your granchildren must be a great comfort to you

Now I hope you wont snub me any longer, but let me have a

friendly line as you used to do.—With my kindest regards to all
your dear circle I remain

Your affectionate f^d

Joseph Severn

[1] Embossed address.

[2] Severn refers to the 1867 biography (see p. 86 n., above), a "Note" in which promises an edition (which did not appear) of the poems "to be printed uniform with this volume." Severn's acknowledgment to Houghton for the 1867 volume will be found in *KC* II, 328.

[3] See p. 83, above, and p. 98, below.

[4] Severn's secretary was Alexander R. Franz. The latter's brother Francesco (see pp. 74–77, above), says Birkenhead, p. 228, in 1868 joined Severn's secretary "and together, when Joseph [Severn] was ill, they stood between him and the outside world, and by stratagem and subterfuge protected him from prying eyes." She also describes (pp. 231, 235) Alexander Franz as British vice-consul at Rome in 1872 (according to John Murray's *Handbook of Rome* [London, 1875], p. 22, his vice-consulate was at 133 Via del Buffalo) and as one of the two trustees appointed in Severn's will.

[5] Shakespeare Wood, the sculptor, was secretary of the British Archaeological Society, John Henry Parker, writer on architecture, its most active member.

[6] See p. 99, below.

⇛ 32 ⇚

JOSEPH SEVERN TO FANNY KEATS DE LLANOS

8 December 1 8 7 0

Envelop addressed: **Madame de Llanos/ cura di Signor Francisco Blanco/** Calle de S. Juan N° 46/ Madrid/ J. S. Rome
Postmarks (partly illegible): ROMA 2 S 9 DIC 70; PD; MA{DRI}D (1) 11 DIC 70.

BRITISH CONSULATE ROME [1]

My dear Mrs de Llanos   Rome 8th Decr 1870

    I have just [read] your very interesting letter which is
a joy to me, for I had written twice & Eleanor once without any
answer & in your former note you mention having written to
me, how is this?
    I had the great pleasure to see Luis on his way to Greece &

from him I heard of your well being, but I crave a particular account of all my friends individually

My twins I have lost—Eleanor [2] is married & Arthur just going to be & so I am now alone & just the same as when you left me—the Marriage of Cana not quite finishd as *I* have been nearly finishd with a severe attack of rheumatism, both my hands & feet but after 4 years I am now well recovered

The siege of Rome took away my Italian consulate & half my income & when the Capital come [3] I shall lose the other half unless the F. O. indulges me with a pension,[4] but all my six children are married so I have only to think of myself which I assure you is rather an odd task for [me] as I have always been thinking of others & *never of myself* the task is a novelty *but irksome* for I always feel a longing to have some one to bestow my good will upon [5]

Also now in the change of Rome I have no longer political prisoners to interest me in getting their release which was an object of great interest to me, in these 10 years I had succeeded in liberating 130 respectable persons

So now you'll all consider me as a very dull personage & that I am no longer worthy of a visit from any of you & yet I live in hopes that the charming association of such friends & on such an occasion, may some day be repeated, who knows how or when?

I trust you will write me a longer letter & say how is dear Mr Llanos & my brother brush Giovanni how Rosa & the Countess—Then Brockman I trust to hear is well set up in health again & doing the Banker [6] in good style—then you must inform me of the dear granchildren & how tall they are

I remember when you left the Acqua Marcia was in its infancy—it is just now completed, the pipes are being laid down all over Rome & I have 50 Shares *not yet paying!!* but there is good hope that it will be a good spec [7]

The poor Pope has shut himself upon the Vatican & *will* be a martyr tho' as yet not quite successfull for the King *assumes* to treat His Holiness with great civility, but he will have none of it & *if* the King comes he will find the Vatican *shut* against him What a strange state of things, but the Roman people like the change as they get back all their *numerous exiled relations,* this alone is a great matter against the Papal gov[t]

This year there are very very few English [8] to eat up all the nice things & I had a fine woodcock yes[dy] for one shilling! 'Tis said that the Italian gov[t] is glad at this for the Romans in idleness lodging letting had caused great dearness in everything, now they'll be obliged to take to industry & cease to live on their wives & the English—All kinds of commerce & trade is now springing up & Rome *ought* to be the richest country in the world as nature has been so bountifull, but will it ever be? can any work be ever [9] got out of these lazy bones?

My position is still pleasant if I don['t] die of "nothing to do" if I am able to assume the "dolce fa[r] niente" which I find very hard work my two good Secretaries are still with me & are greatly devoted to me as well as all about me—I shall soon get some of the new married couples—think of six weddings in my family

You only write "Madrid" so I will direct this to Sig Blanco, for I am afraid of losing you again tho' Luis assurd me that I had got your right address—With my sincere love to all your charming circle beleive me

Your affectionate f[d]

Joseph Severn

[1] Embossed address.

[2] Born in 1841, she married Henry Furneaux, Fellow of Corpus Christi, Oxford, in May, 1870.

[3] Pope Pius IX had surrendered Rome on September 20; it became the capital of the new kingdom of Italy on July 1, 1871, and the king, Victor Emmanuel, entered the next day, taking up his residence at the Quirinal Palace.

[4] On his pension from the Foreign Office see p. 94, below.

[5] See his statement on p. 85, above, and p. 95, below.

[6] See p. 84, above.

[7] See p. 83, above.

[8] John Murray's *Handbook of Rome* (1875) says that in 1870 there "were only

457 resident Protestants" in Rome, and the number of English people must have been much smaller.

⁹ *Written* every.

⇶ 33 ⇷

JOSEPH SEVERN TO FANNY KEATS DE LLANOS

24 February 1871

Envelop addressed: Mrs de Llanos/ Calle de Lope de Vega N° 61/ Madrid/ J. Severn

Postmarks: ROMA 8 S 24 FEB 71; PD; T{U}RINO 6 R 26 FEB. . .

BRITISH CONSULATE. ROME [1]

Rome 24 Feb. 1871

My dear Mrs de Llanos

   Yest^y I answerd your telegram "that Horace Flacchi lives at the Consulta Monte Cavallo" [2] & I hope you received it

   My answer to your kind letter of the 23^d ult has been delayd on account of immensity of care caused by [3] the frigh[t]full inundation which now begins to be passed over the poor Romans having received in kind (new) all that they had lost— My country people, few as they are gave 10 thousand f^{cs}; indeed the charity has [4] abounded & the Roma[n]s behaved really well under their affliction [5]

   You ask who the Lady is my dear boy Arthur is about to marry? She is Miss Joan Agnew a ward of the famous John Ruskin the great Art Critic & I have reason to be much gratified, not only as he bestows a charming & well to do Bride on my Son; [6] but also as he considers Arthur a great genius & another Turner

   Have I not been happy in my dear children altho' I am now left alone—yet soon no doubt I shall have dozens of granchildren tumbling aye & perhaps great granchildren!! for my eldest grandaughter is now 17

   It seems that on the Capital in June coming to Rome [7] that

my poor [pension] will be swallowd up, but on good authority
I shall get a pension if Mr Gladstones "cutting down" will admit
of it

I am glad to tell that I am not only well recovered but
"groun'd so young" that all the Anglo Roman world is going to
my Tolfa [8] to be ground also & I confess to you that I have not
wrinkle or frown, but I dont know how to turn my "looks" to
account for this is the 50th year since I came to Rome with your
illustrious brother!!!

You dont mention my dear & gifted friend Rosa, do tell me
about her & her splendid music which still is running in my
memory so charmingly—How often I feel the loss of you all for
you most indulgently made me as one of yourselves—You'll
remember Miss Novello,[9] she is now staying with me & has a
most dear recollection of you all & begs to be most kindly placed
in your memories & I the same with the hope that we may still
meet in dear old Rome altho it is now going thro such queer
transformation—What will come of the two kings in the *one*
city? [10]

Yours affectionately

Joseph Severn

[1] Embossed address.

[2] The Palazzo della Consulta on Monte Cavallo in 1871 was attached to the
Quirinal Palace for the use of the court.

[3] *Written* but.

[4] *Written* has has.

[5] S. W. Halperin, *Italy and the Vatican at War* (Chicago, 1939), p. 146: "On
December 27 [1870] the Tiber rose and flooded half of Rome . . . The destruc-
tion of life and property horrified the entire country, and aid for the destitute
was at once organized on a national scale."

[6] Joseph Arthur Palliser Severn (died February 23, 1931) married Joan
Ruskin Agnew (died June 27, 1924), cousin and ward of Ruskin, in 1871.

[7] It came on July 1: see p. 90 n., above.

[8] That is, to the baths of Tolfa, twenty miles from Rome. See pp. 94, 100, below.

[9] Emma Novello, a daughter of Keats's acquaintance, Vincent Novello. A letter
of hers to Mme. Llanos is in the Paradinas collection.

[10] Meaning the "imprisoned" pope, Pius IX, and the king, Victor Emmanuel.

-≫ 34 ≪-

JOSEPH SEVERN TO FANNY KEATS DE LLANOS
9 May 1872

Address: Madame Keats de Llanos/ Calle de Lope de Vega N° 61/
Madrid/ J. Severn
Postmarks: ROMA 10 MAG 72 10 M; PD; TORINO . . . 11 MAG 72
10 ½ S; MADRID (1) 15 MAY 72

Rome 9th May 1872

My dear Mrs de Llanos

I crave pardon for my tardy answer to your last letter—
but I have lived in such a continued turmoil with the breaking
up of my Consulate & the striving for a pension & so on, that I
have not had courage to write till now

First I will answer your questions—as regards the invention
of Count Brockman for the bridge twixt Dover & Calais & if I
can give him introductions to further this object: I beg to assure
him that my Son Walter will do any thing & every thing He is
in the Privy Council office & I trust the Count may remember
him

Next if I met your Son Johns friend and s[c]hoolfellow? he
paid me a visit & I was much pleased to hear news of you all
from so excellent a person, but I dare say before this he must
be returned to Spain

And now about Rome—'tis indeed changed for an inundation of Italian strangers have helpd to double the population &
every place of profit has fallen into their hands—the stately
Roman is beat out of the field—Rome is filld with fine shops
that seem almost ball rooms so that the dear old place you'd
hardly know again   The Italian Bible is selling in the streets,
bound gilt & letterd for a franc   Newspapers are hawked about
all day the houses have doubled in their rents & every thing

increased in price *three fold*—how the poor live I cannot guess

The good things are the numerous schools & tis interesting to see how the Roman children *devour* education—in this I see the downfall of the Papacy—There is no end to building

As regards myself I am still in the same house or rather in the part looking over the fountain of Trevi, all the rest is let & the large saloon is occupied by the Archaeological society,[1] in this I was so fortunate as to "sot me down" rent free—My pension is a scanty affair £140 a year,[2] but I have my painting to fall back upon—The severe attack of rheumatism I have had for 7 years has made my painting languish, but I am now well cured, tho' my hands are sadly "out of drawing"—Now that all my children are married I am left somewhat alone & feel at times my loneliness irksome, indeed I thought of returning to England to be in the midst of my children & granchildren 16 in number, but the Doctors assure me that one English winter would cripple me for life for I cannot stand damp or cold

How I wish you & Mr Llanos would come & take part of my house with me & let us begin again "da capo" for those happy days we passed together I am always dwelling on & more so now

Sir Augustus Paget an English minister is here [3] but the Pope wont receive him—I often hear dear Rosas music in my memory & the singing of the charming Countess, then John & I communicate on painting

My picture of the marriage of Cana is not quite finishd, but wanting but little, it gets me great praises & certainly rewards me for the immence labours I bestowd up[on it.]

I am just expecting my son Arthur & his Bride with a party of 8 friends, they'll stay only a fortnight!! during 6 summers I have been to a mountain town (Tolfa) for the baths, 'tis 12 miles from Civita Vecchia

With my sincere love to all your party not forgetting your dear granchildren I remain your

sincere f^d Joseph Severn

Lord Houghton is producing a splendid edition of the life &

works of your illustrious brother [4] & I am expecting a Photo
from America [5] from a drawing of mine [6]

[1] See p. 87, above.
[2] £80 was his official Foreign Office pension, £60 came from the Civil List.
[3] Paget was ambassador to the new capital.
[4] *The Poetical Works of John Keats. With a Memoir* (revised edition, London, 1871).
[5] Probably from Emma Keats (Mrs. Philip) Speed or her son, John Gilmer Speed.
[6] This postscript is written at the head of the letter.

→≫ 35 ≪←

JOSEPH SEVERN TO FANNY KEATS DE LLANOS
28 May 1873

Address: To/ M[rs] Keats de Llanos/ J. Severn/ by His Excellency [1]

Rome 28th May 1873

My dear M[rs] Llanos

'Twas a joy to me meeting Lewis & to hear of his present
appointment, which if it [2] endures & he remains he gives me
hope that you may all return to old Rome once more—Altho' I
confess that I am comfortable this would complete my happiness
  I dare say you know that I am no longer Consul & that I am
"giubilato"; so now I have to tell you that I am in the strange
position of having only to think of myself which to me is
somewhat odd & even uncomfortable [3]—all my 6 children are
married & well doing in England & I should have had nothing
but my rheumatism if I had not been so lucky as to get rid of it
  You & I may now count up our granchildren you with five &
I with eighteen but you have the advantage of seeing yours every
day whereas I have only seen two of mine as yet & scarcely know
when I shall get a visit from the rest
  Eleanor has a son & daughter & Arthur a daughter only—
these my twins are both most admirably married, indeed I

may say the same of all the others & I assure you that I feel myself to be really fortunate in thus (tho' a poor Artist) haveing been enabled to do so much for my dear ones

I am still in the old Poli but the Prince my Landlord has now divided the Palace, made me a new & easy stair case at the Sala [4] Dante & so that ugly tiresome old entrance I have done with & the rooms over the Fountain of Trevi I have let to the Philodramatic Society who are making a fine Theatre,—they took me by surprise with such a liberal offer that I am *actually now rent free*

You'll think of me in my loneliness but this also has come to an end for my good Doctor of Tolfa with his wife & sister [5] are now keeping house with me & so I am very comfortable & well lookd after for even this last may be essential as this year I shall be in my 80th year!! but as yet I dont show any sign of decay & am so possessed with a youthfulness of soul that as I was a great invalid in my early days; so now in a certain way I seem to be enjoying my youth

The rheumatism of which after 7 years fighting I am right well cured, has not left any ugliness except my hands being *sadly out of drawing*—but I can paint & write & do every thing except my piano forte playing which I assure you is very so so Lewis gives me a good account of you all even to your Vine-yards—that Count Brockman is quite recovered & dear Rosa brilliant as ever at her Music

I never pass up the Via Gregoriana [6] without seeing you all in my minds eye & thinking over the many charming days & evenings I have passed there

Nothing like the same tranquility have we now, for Rome is risen up into the busy world & is just now doing away with the 400 Monasteries & Convents by a Parliamentary vote of 196 against 46   what a change!!! & what will it come to?[7] I cannot beleive it yet as I am so used to the old state of things—L[y] Castle Stuart [8] is still up at Monte Maria & is the only Roman Antique unchanged

With my love to all your circle beleive
Yours Sincerly,
Joseph Severn

[1] Probably sent by British Embassy mail.
[2] *Apparently* ift.
[3] See pp. 85, 89, above.
[4] One might suppose it to be the Sala di Dante (Sala Dantesca), behind the Fontana di Trevi, a large hall, decorated with subjects from the *Divine Comedy*, for concerts and other entertainments. But on August 5, 1877 (see No. 37), he gives his address as "Scala Dante," and Birkenhead, p. 230, remarks: "You entered the huge Palazzo Poli and climbed the steps of the Scala Dante."
[5] The Valerianis. The sister, Margherita, died in March, 1875; the doctor Severn made one of the two trustees of his estate and the recipient of all his Keats manuscripts (Birkenhead, pp. 233, 235).
[6] A street leading to the top of the Spanish Steps.
[7] A change not mentioned in S. W. Halperin's *Italy and the Vatican at War* (Chicago, 1939).
[8] See pp. 80, 83f., above. Since her father married in 1805 and died in 1809 she was probably around sixty-seven years old.

→≫ 36 ≪←

JOSEPH SEVERN TO FANNY KEATS DE LLANOS
15 July 1873

Rome 15th July 1873

My dear M[rs] Llanos

Yours of the 11th inst brought me much charming intelligence & very dear enquiries

I confess I was most agreably surprised at seeing dear Luis & at his splendid position but I regret that he seems not well establishd in it as you anticipate in your letter but yet I hope some good will come of it when the Spanish gov[t] is well set up— But there is such an ugly fashion sprung up for confusion

You kindly enquire who my dear Eleanor married—A M[r] Furneau,[1] a great Oxford Rev[d]—she has two children & has made a very favorable & happy marriage

Arthur also the like, he is married to a Miss Agnew & pursues his painting tho' I'm afraid he is too comfortable to make much of it, for in addition to his Wifes fortune the late Duke of Bedford [2] left him an annuity   all this is very bad for an artist but as he has very fine talents perhaps he'll do well

You will be pleasd to hear that I am once more *actually* at my darling pursuit & have done two pictures since I last wrote you [3]

The other day I had the pleasure to dine with Louis & his nice wife at the Palaz Spagna [4]—I was delighted with them both, but Louis has always been a great favorite of mine & I cannot but think favorably of his future for he seems born to fortune

I regret to hear that dear John (my brother brush) does not do much, but I fear that in the midst of so much political hubbub his mind is disturbed

My hope is greater inasmuch as Louis succeeding, you and M[r] Llanos may come again to Rome

The Acqua Marcia is going on well in every thing, except paying interest [5]   Yours Sincerly

                                        Joseph Severn

My warm regards to all your dear ones

[1] Really Furneaux: see p. 90 n., above.

[2] William Russell (1809–1872), the eleventh duke, a complete recluse, whose personality was under £600,000.

[3] He can hardly mean since May 28. One may have been "Isabella and the Pot of Basil" (see p. 100, below), which on September 24, 1874, he referred to as "my new picture" (Birkenhead, p. 231). The other may have been one of his numerous pictures of Keats.

[4] The Palazzo di Spagna, on the west side of the Piazza di Spagna, had been the Spanish embassy since the seventeenth century.

[5] See p. 85 n., above.

→»» 37 «««-

JOSEPH SEVERN TO FANNY KEATS DE LLANOS[1]
5 August 1877

Envelop addressed: Madam Fanny Keats de Llanos/ 5 Calle di Lista/
Madrid/ J. Severn Rome
Postmarks (imperfect): ROM . . . FERROVI . . . 6 8–77 6 S: MADRID
(1) 10 AGO 77

Rome—Scala Dante
5th August 1877

My dear Madam de Llanos

It is a joy to me to get a letter from you for we have been
so long separated by wars & revolutions that I imagine you had
a heap of trouble

Your friend J. I. Vilar *did* come & I had the pleasure of an
hours chat with him & he gave me your new address [2]—I had
also heard of you & yours from the Sect[y] of the Spanish Embassy
who informed me that your Louis was about to visit Rome
again, *but* as *you do not mention* it I doubt it. Also you [do]
not tell me about dear Rosa

My painting languishes a little no doubt owing to my 84
years, yet my eyesight is excellent and [3] my hand steady & *my
impudence is great,* my marriage of Cana is just done after 10
years,[4] but as I have sufferd severely at times from rheumatism;
so I have been much interupted & now I look at the picture
with wonderment & delight that I could have gone on with it
to the end—dear Rosa [5] is still the best figure amongst the 20

Another draw back has been the malevolent attacks at me as
Consul, even to killing me of—but I had more talent than any
of them & as I never lose my temper, they were defeated, these
6 Englishmen—now that there is an Ambassadour I have 2
pensions (I put one in each eye) & am very comfortable keeping
house with an excellent Doctor & his wife—but my Poli has been
cut in half & I have a good stair case

I took 75 baths of the Tolfa boiling spring & so I am well set up

Just now I am beginning a life size portrait of the illustrious Poet [6] & I receive continued communications [7] about him— His fame is much [*illegible word*] & last year Gen Sir Vincent Eyre erected a new tomb to his memory [8]

But to your interesting request, that I would strive for a pension for you, this I will do with all my heart but Mr Gladstone not being in office I think there is difficulty but I will also try Lord Houghton [9]

My children are a great happiness to me & sometimes visit me, I have 25 granchildren Eleanor has 3 & is really well married & the same of Arthur who has also 3 children & is very successfull as an artist, indeed I am very happy in my children, but I lost my gifted Mary & also Claudia

How glad I am that you have 6 granchildren but I am grieved that you have to mount 4 pair of stairs [10] because I remember you were weak in your knees & it must be hard for you

That your Leopold is director of a railway [11] I am not a little glad

Do tell me about dear John, is he able to pursue his art? I am afraid not—There are here pensioned Spanish students greatly distinguishing themselves

I conclude with assuring you that I am very comfortable, & beg to be most kindly rem[em]bered to Mr Llanos & all your dear ones

beleive me yours very sincerely

Joseph Severn

PS a picture of Isabella & the pot of Basil I have just done

---

[1] A reply, in a very shaky hand, to Fanny Llanos' letter of July 27 printed by Sharp, pp. 252f. On "Scala Dante" see p. 97 n., above.

[2] Fanny wrote that "a Spanish friend of ours . . . tells me that he called upon you; but had not the pleasure of seeing you, as you were at the time taking your siesta."

[3] *Written* any.

[4] Or rather fifteen years: see p. 80, above.

[5] See p. 84, above.

[6] "His last picture was of Keats" (Birkenhead, p. 236).

[7] *Apparently* communtions.

[8] Eyre merely restored the old tomb (1875) with money sent him by Mary Frere, of London, and Emma Keats Speed, of Louisville. He also raised further money to place a marble medallion of Keats (1875) in the Protestant Cemetery, Rome, and a marble tablet (1879) on the wall of the house in which Keats died (*KC* II, 342f., 355–357, 369–371). See also p. 105, below.

[9] See p. 100, above. On the outcome of Houghton's and H. B. Forman's efforts to get a pension for her see Adami, pp. 190–196.

[10] In her letter Fanny said, "We have unfortunately gone down in the world, and up to a fourth floor" (5, Calle de Lista).

[11] Count Brockmann had recently been made Director of the Railways of Jerez and Sanlúcar. He died in 1878 (Adami, p. 176).

-≫ 38 ≪-

SIR CHARLES W. DILKE TO FANNY KEATS DE LLANOS
1 2 February 1 8 7 8

76. Sloane Street. S.W.[1]
12 February 1878

Dear Madame Llanos

Not being quite sure of your address I write to you in this Post by duplicate sending one letter to an address which has been given to me, and one through my friend the Spanish Minister.

A Mr Forman has published, very much against my wish, those of the letters which he has (not those which I have) [2] which passed between your Brother John and Miss Brawne. On hearing from you I will if you like send you a copy of the publication through the post.[3]

You have I believe a portrait of your Brother by Severn. Could you very kindly describe to me its size & attitude and whether it is in water colors and on ivory. Also whether it was painted by Severn from your Brother or painted from one of the others after your Brother's death. I have the one which was painted for Miss Brawne, and two copies from it. [4]

Y[rs] very truly

Charles W. Dilke

[1] Embossed address.

[2] A very interesting remark. Later he wrote (Stephen Gwynn and Gertrude M. Tuckwell, *The Life of the Rt. Hon. Sir Charles W. Dilke* [London, 1917], II, 543): "About this time (1878) Mr. Buxton Forman announced for publication the Keats Love-Letters, which I certainly thought I had in a vague way bought for the purpose of preventing publication. They had been long in my possession, but the son of Fanny Brawne had claimed them, and I, having no written agreement, had found it necessary to give them up—although what I had bought and paid for, unless it was the right to prevent publication, I do not know." The remark above makes it clear that Sir Charles did *not* surrender all the letters. Those he retained were in all likelihood among the Keats letters that his secretary, Mr. H. K. Hudson (see Joanna Richardson, *Fanny Brawne* [London, 1952], p. 169), saw him burn.

[3] On March 19 he wrote to Mme. Llanos, "I have ordered a copy of the Keats love-letters to be sent to you." Forman also sent her a copy on April 30, and in a letter of May 9 (now in the Harvard Paradinas collection) he warmly defended his motives in publishing the book.

[4] A photograph, made around 1890 by F. Holland Day, of the letter in which Fanny Brawne Lindon offered to sell this miniature to C. W. Dilke, is in the Harvard Keats Collection, and the original is quoted by George C. Williamson, *The Keats Letters, Papers, and Other Relics Forming the Dilke Bequest in the Hampstead Public Library* (London, 1914). The miniature which Sir Charles called "the only original and the only undoubted Severn" is now in the National Portrait Gallery. His two copies of it are in the Fitzwilliam Museum, Cambridge, and the Keats-Shelley House, Rome. See Williamson, pp. 99–101.

EMMA FRANCES KEATS SPEED TO FANNY
KEATS DE LLANOS

7 April 1 8 7 8

Louisville April 7th

My Dear Aunt Fanny

Through a paragraph in an English paper, I learn that you are ill and suffering; [1] I am so grieved to hear it, and I hasten to write begging for information as to your health—If you are unable to write yourself will you get one of your children to do so—I am so drawn to you by the ties of blood that I feel an interest in all that concerns you and yours—I was unable because of sickness to go to the Centennial Exposition, thereby losing the pleasure of seeing my cousin's picture.[2] My son who lives in Philadelphia tells me that he showed it to some Amateurs in painting who spoke in praise of its excellence. I fear you did not receive my last letter, you have been heretofore so kind and prompt in your replies. Probably I failed to give the proper address. Having never beheld any kindred except Father and Mother and their descendants the desire to see you and yours increases with my years. I wish you would send me a photograph of yourself or of your children or of both, nothing would be more valued by me. I read a little sketch of your young Queen's school days, that she was your queen added interest to the article [3]—I saw by the papers that you naturally disapproved the publication of the 'Keats Love Letters' [4] Since they were not published by his own family or with their consent, I do not regret, for not one of the letters fails to increase our respect and admiration for him, he seems, ⟨to have⟩ with his pure sensitive spirit to have detected the unlovely qualities of the woman, although he was immovably constant to the last— His death may have been to him a merciful release—I saw in a

picture dealers a very prettily conceived picture of "Isabel the
pot of basil"—The engraving is a coarse one but spirited; I
liked it so well that I bought it and it is being framed to hang
up over the little miniatures of your two brothers. May I not
have one of you to add to the group—My husband and children
send love—We hope soon to hear of your good health. My
address is '228 First street' Please give my regards to my uncle—

With respect

I am your affectionate

Niece

Fanny Keats Speed

[1] The *Athenaeum*, March 23, 1878, p. 383, wrote of Señora Llanos: "At an
advanced age, and when her health is impaired, she finds herself reduced to
poverty by unexpected misfortunes." It suggested that the Prime Minister grant
her a pension from the Civil List.

[2] The Philadelphia exposition ran from May through November, 1876. According to the *Exposicion Internacional en Filadelfia de 1876* (Madrid, 1876),
p. 111, Juan Llanos was represented by "Un cuadro al óleo."

[3] Alphonso XII early in 1878 married Princess Maria de las Mercedes, who
died six months later.

[4] The *Athenaeum*, March 23, 1878, p. 383, said: "Madame Llanos . . . has
written to her friends in England expressing strong disapproval of the publication of her brother's love-letters." See also Adami, pp. 182–190. Mrs. Speed
later changed her opinion. She wrote to her Aunt Fanny on October 28, 1878:
"Uncle John's letters were very very sad, but I think ought never to have been
published—The publisher [Charles Welford?] wrote to me for information
concerning Fanny Braun, and it seemed strange ⟨to me⟩ for I am told he is a
cousin of that lady, who by the way, was not the least fitted to have been the
companion of John Keats with his ardent sensitive nature."

⇥⟫ 40 ⟪⇤

EMMA FRANCES KEATS SPEED[1] TO FANNY
KEATS DE LLANOS[2]

25 May 1879

Envelop addressed: Madame Fanny de Llanos/ 5. Calle de Lista/ Barrio
de Salamanca/ Madrid/ Spain
Postmarks: LOUISVILLE KY MAY 28 11 AM; CARTER 12 JUN 7{9};
MADRID (1) 12 JUN 79

Louisville May 25th 1879

My Dear Aunt Fanny

    Just as I received your letter of May 2nd I was thinking of
writing to our Minister in Spain to beg of him to find your
whereabouts—your letter relieved my apprehensions. You [3] will
not be surprised when I tell you that poor Mother is dead—She
was laid at rest in our Cemetery on the 17th of April [4]—Her death
was peaceful and unsuffering—I went to Lexington to her—she
was pleased to have me with her—she was attended by an excellent nurse, my sisters Alice and Ella and her husband M^r
Jeffrey—I send you a notice of her death taken from the New
York Sun [5]—I noticed the little sum [6] which was given you by
the Bounty Fund, it ought to have been a pension—I was very
much disappointed, for a year ago I saw that it had been
recommended to the Government—and hoped for something
liberal—I will send you a pleasant notice of the ceremony of
unvailing the tablet placed over the door of the residence of
Keats [7]—It provokes me that all the papers insist that the grave
of Keats was restored by private subscription—A * friend of mine
living in Rome attended to the work which was done at a
trifling cost—I sent her the money and now have the receipt for
it [8]—Twenty five dollars of mine were still in my friend's hands,
this money she appropriated for the tablet over the door—I love
to hear of my cousins and of their children—of their studies,
and of their cheerful efforts to assist one another—It seems hard

where the families are so small that the Ocean should separate them—I wish I might have pictures of my cousins they would be very precious to me, one of yourself would be placed with my most precious possessions—We have an English acquaintance here the son of an Ex Mayor of Liverpool who is well acquainted with Warrington Wood, the Sculptor of the bust of Keats; he promises to write to him asking the price of a plaster cast— [9] I will let you know in my next all about it—I have one son living in New York who is employed on the New York World [10] —He is the only one of my children who is at all gifted; the others are sensible, nice affectionate and industrious—Please write soon—Fanny, Florence, and Tom send love to all of you— Mr S. desires his remembrances—

Your affectionate niece

Fanny Keats Speed

* Miss Clarke of Boston

[1] Mrs. Philip Speed.

[2] Who endorsed it in pencil: "Speaks of our family."

[3] *Written* your.

[4] Georgiana Wylie Keats, who married John Jeffrey on January 5, 1843, died in Lexington, Kentucky, on April 3 and, according to the *Courier-Journal*, was buried in the Philip Speed lot, Cave Hill Cemetery, Louisville, on April 7.

[5] See *KC* I, cii f.

[6] Of £150: see Adami, pp. 194f.

[7] See *KC* II, 355–357, 369–371.

[8] According to General Sir Vincent Eyre, the money used for restoring the tomb was provided jointly by Mary Frere, daughter of the statesman Sir Bartle Frere, and Mrs. Speed (see *KC* II, 342, and p. 100, above). Ednah Dow Cheney, *Reminiscences* (Boston, 1902), p. 146, calls Sarah Freeman Clarke, "an exquisite landscape painter," "the only pupil of Allston," and tells how she left Italy to live (and die) in Georgia, where she founded the Atlanta Public Library and worked to help the Negroes.

[9] Wood made at his own cost, not a bust, but the marble medallion of Keats that is placed on the wall by the entrance to Keats's and Severn's graves (see p. 101 n., above). Wood, whose studio was in the Villa Campana, near St. John Lateran, was famous at that time for his "Recumbent Eve" and for the heroic group, "St. Michael Conquering Satan," he had made for his fellow-townsmen of Warrington, Lancashire.

[10] John Gilmer Speed (1853–1909), managing editor of the *World*, 1879–1883, who edited Keats's letters and poems in 1883 (3 vols., New York).

APPENDIX

JOHN TAYLOR TO JOSEPH SEVERN
6 February 1 8 2 1

Address: Joseph Severn Esq/ Poste restant/ Rome
Postmarks: ANGLETERRE; CHAMBERY; F 21 137 (*twice*)

London 6 Febry 1821

My dear Sir,

The very distressing State in which my poor Friend lies,
and in which his Illness plunges you, would at any time afflict
me very sensibly, but I feel more than I can express when I
hear that my precautions (which were only taken for Keats's
advantage) have proved a Source of so great Unquiet as your
letter to Haslam exhibits.[1]—Surely my Letter which was sent
off at the same Time that Dr Clarke was written to[2] must have
miscarried, or it is unopened, or lying at the Post Office—You
would have seen by it that all my Doubts [?] were so guarded
from leading to your Inconvenience that except for a few Days
suspence you could not be materially affected—I was afraid if
all the money was to go away at once by one of my good Friend
Keats's generous Impulses, he would have none left to depend
upon.—But that being ascertained not to be the case all will go
on as usual. The Bill will be paid on the day it becomes due
which I believe is the 18th Inst—and Torlonia's will not only let
you have the rest of the money, which I hope is done ere this,
but you may further draw upon us for Fifty Pounds more (as
I told Dr Clarke in my last Letter, and after that if necessary for
50£ more still—Most earnestly do I pray to God to bless our
dear Friend Keats with Peace, his Peace that nothing earthly
can take away, and often do I wish that I was with you if it was
only to relieve you from some of your Fatigues & Cares, but I
should also try to pray with and converse with Keats, in the
Hope of being enabled by those Means to render his Illness less

oppressive—You have been in a wonderful Manner enabled to perform all your Duties to him and they have been of the utmost Service to our dear Friend:—in this Thought you will find Comfort at a future Day which not all the happiness of your past Life can equal.—If Keats is well enough to allow of your reading to him I wish you would go through the Book of Job. He will admire it for its Poetry; but he will also, with his Spirit which so deeply searches, discern that it is a most important Lesson which it teaches us. When the Spirits of Goodness & of Evil presented themselves at the Throne of God, & the latter by God's permission was suffered to try Job, ⟨t⟩he ⟨latter⟩ bore his afflictions with great Patience not even in his Heart raising up himself against the Judgment of God—no not though his wife would have made him impatient of God's Dominion, renouncing it as if it could not be, now that he was persecuted who had done no wrong.—More to vex & harrass him his 3 Friends all declared their Conviction that he must be a Hypocrite and secretly a Sinner, and advised him to repent that he might escape the Wrath due to wicked Men.—But Job made a Declaration of Integrity such as few could equal him in—& so far he did no wrong—But when he wishes to hear what the Lord could allege against him, when he desires to plead his Cause against the hard Decree of the Almighty Judge, arrogating to himself that he knew himself thoroughly & could not err in his opinion of himself; then God by the Voice of Elihu caused him to know the difference between the thing created & its Creator, & by the infinite Distance which he proved to be between them he shewed Job his Error. Then Job confessed that nothing can be pure in the Sight of God,—that nothing can maintain itself against his Power,—that the clay knows nothing of its own Nature compared to the knowledge of him who moulds it as it pleases him— He admitted the Impropriety of his Defence, & submitted himself & his Reward in a worldly sense was said to be great, but in a future State would be infinitely above Comparison with what was his Lot before he was afflicted.—I feel a strong & confident

Hope in God that our dear Keats will be blessed with Job's Reward—and if he could bear to hear the Story it might not only amuse but confirm his Mind.—

I requested (by a Friend) that Dr Clarke would provide you with whatever might be necessary, if Torlonia's withheld th{e} Money in Consequence of my previous Inquiry about the Bi{ll} —and I wrote to Dr Clarke stating it would be paid a for{tnight} since; besides my Letter to Keats of the earlier Date. I wi{ll en}deavour therefore to persuade myself that you were not long in a State of Misery about this Business.—Do not let any of K's papers be destroyed [3]—& be under no apprehensions respecting anything else.—Reynolds sent 50£ a fortnight since Did you receive it [4]—you must open such Letters as those which you suspect are not from one only Friend of K's—Miss B. [5]

I saw a Letter from a Female Cousin [6] of mine in Cincinnati yesterday, who says that she has been at Louisville paying a Visit at Mr George Keats's—She describes them as very happy, living very comfortably, and only desirous of getting back to England as soon as they can make it convenient to retire from the Business he is embarked in—

I fear you can hardly read my writing—but the only Satisfactory Part of it, the assurance of the Bill being paid, & your consequent Relief from all Trouble on that head, with the Request that you will draw for 50 or 100£ more if necessary will be more sure to meet your Eye if I repeat it

Pray tell Dr Clarke that I feel very grateful to him for the kind Interest he takes.—Assure Keats of my Heart's sincerest Sympathy with him—and accept my dear Sir the warm though unavailing best wishes & prayers of yours Ever truly

John Taylor

[1] On January 15 (*KC* I, 195–200) Severn, who had drawn £150 at one time on Taylor and Hessey, wrote to Haslam, "To[r]lonia's—the bankers—have refused any more money—the bill is returned unaccepted—'no effects.'"

[2] This comment makes it probable that Dr. James Clark's letter of January 3, preserved only in a partial, unaddressed transcript by Hessey (*KC* I, 185f.), was written to Taylor or to an employee of his.

[3] Later Severn "sent the most valuable literary remains," not to Taylor, but to Charles Brown (Sharp, p. 108).

[4] On April 3, Taylor told Severn (Sharp, p. 100), "Reynolds, I find, did not send the £50 after all. I did not know that till very lately; he wrote [to me of his] desire Keats would draw upon him for that sum."

[5] See the identical warning about Fanny Brawne's letters that Brown sent to Severn on January 15 (*KC* I, 201).

[6] Mary Taylor, wife of Michael Drury (see p. 45, above).

→》》 42 《《←

J. A. HESSEY TO JOSEPH SEVERN[1]

1 2 February 1 8 2 1

Address: Joseph Severn Esq/ Post Office/ Rome
Postmarks: F 10[. . .] [2] 21; CHAMBERY; ANGLETERRE; 3 MARZO

London Feb. 12. 1821

My dear Sir

The harrowing Accounts which you have sent us of the state of our poor friend Keats induce me to write to you in the hope, however forlorn it may be, of imparting something like comfort to him and you, if it be not too late. Would to God it were in my power to give him that peace of mind which he so much needs in this his hour of trial. Our poor friend enquires, you say, "why he cannot possess that cheap comfort which every fool may have" [3]—alas, my dear Sir, its very cheapness has been the stumbling block to him—yet it is cheap though of the utmost value, and as we have the highest authority for saying "ask and ye shall receive, seek and ye shall find," let me beg you to urge him to *ask that he may have.* Has he ever prayed for Heavenly Consolation?—Does he pray for it?—It cannot be had without praying for, and O may God give him the heart to pray, and may He graciously receive his Prayers. But what, he will perhaps say am I to pray for?—for Pardon of his Sins, and for Acceptance through Jesus Christ—Alas, I fear this is a Name he knows but little of—and I sincerely wish it were in my power effectually to introduce it to his notice. Our friend is too sensible, too wise, to suppose there is *no God*—or that God is not good—and being, as He is, all goodness, God must hate all evil. God has given us his Laws to obey, under Penalty of Punishment beyond what we can conceive—we have all disobeyed His laws, and rendered ourselves liable to that Punishment—God has also proclaimed his Offer of Pardon and of unspeakable eternal happiness, and He has prescribed the Terms on which alone he will grant it— Jesus Christ, the eternal Son of God came into this world, took our Nature upon him, fulfilled the Divine law in his own person, and suffered Death as a propitiation for the sins of all mankind. By virtue of his atonement Pardon is freely offered to all who, repenting of their Sins, will pray to God for Pardon through him and by Faith in him. How simple, how beautifully simple is this System of Scriptural Truth which Infidels cannot or will not comprehend. A just God proclaims his Anger against all Sin,—a merciful God will pardon all Sin for the Sake of a divine Mediator. He that will seek for pardon thro' this Mediator, feeling his want of it, and believing in the willingness of God to grant it through Him, shall be freely pardoned— The Spirit of God will purify his Heart and Life, and make him fit for the enjoyment of Heavenly Happiness. O that our dear friend may be enabled earnestly and heartily to pray for this pardon, this comfort, this preparation of the heart, and may his passage out of this life be to a happy Eternity.

But you will say, Keats is too ill, too weak to be spoken to on such subjects, or to be reasoned with—it will agitate him too much.—My dear Sir, he is not too ill to be very unhappy—his time is very short—and a word in season may make him happy eternally—Were I sitting by his bedside I certainly should not read him the lecture which I have just written to you.—I should watch my opportunity, and when I heard his complaints would say, "My dear Keats, there *is* a God—*do pray to Him for relief*— he is *Almighty* and he *can* relieve you—he is *merciful* and he _will_ relieve you—he has _commanded_ us to pray to him, and _he will answer_ our prayers—he has appointed a _Saviour,_ for whose sake he _will accept us."_—A few words like these, affectionately spoken, and _marked with Sincerity,_ have, I speak from experience, much more effect than reasoning—And when a man feels the insufficiency of this world's Philosophy to make him happy, a word of Heavenly Wisdom is Heaven itself to his Heart. Do but get him to _pray_—to feel that _there may be some use_ in praying—to utter _but one earnest prayer_ from the heart and you may then have hope. "Lord be merciful to me a Sinner"—"Lord I believe, help thou mine unbelief"—may bring down mercy and Peace into his Heart, and give him a degree of happiness which he has never yet known. For my own Part, so convinced am I of the truth of what I have been saying that I would not for worlds think otherwise—It has been my daily Prayer for poor Keats, ever since I heard of his Illness, that it might please God to enlighten his understanding and to change his Heart— I thought I could do no more—Yet this one expedient suggested itself—it occurred to me that I might possibly convey a useful hint to you & him, & that it might be blessed, humble as it is. But alas! it may arrive too late—my letter may find you mourning over the loss of your friend—if so, God grant, that he may not h{ave need}ed my assistance, but that a change may have been wroug{ht in his} heart before he left this world, and that he may have entered into that "rest which remaineth for the People of God."

To you, my dear friend, the Scenes which you must have witnessed have been awful lessons—may they sink deep into your heart. You may not have thought much on such subjects before—they have been forced on your Notice now, and let me be excused when I strongly and earnestly recommend them to your serious attention. I am but a poor divine, and am perhaps going beyond my province in thus addressing you—but your affectionate attentions to my poor friend Keats have made me feel towards you as a _friend,_ and with the freedom of a friend I venture to address you. Think deeply on these things—Search the Scriptures and see if I have not spoken the words of Truth & Soberness—it is not Cant believe me. We cannot tell how soon you & I may need the same kind Offices which you are paying to Keats, and how soon we may be compelled to call in the aid of all our Religious faith for Consolation on our Death bed. O may our hope be fixed on that firm foundation which shall never fail us. You have seen that Worldly Philosophy will not support a Man at such an hour and as such an hour must come it is madness not to be prepared for it. May it be your happy lot, and mine, to meet it with composure, with hope, with faith, with Confidence—There is but one way by which we can so meet it, and may we be enabled to know and to follow it. Once more let me apologize for this long letter, and beg you to receive & understand it as it is meant—Make my most affectionate regards to my dear friend Keats—I wish I could entertain hopes of his recovery, but as that I fear is hopeless I hope to meet him in a happier world where sorrow shall be no more. You will not of course I suppose shew or read this to him as I understand he cannot bear to hear letters from his friends—but make use of it according to your Discretion and may a blessing attend it— Farewell, My dear Sir—may you be supported under all your trials & succeed in all your wishes

Believe me, very sincerely Your friend

J. A. Hessey

let me hear from you soon

[1] Sharp, p. 86, saw this letter and referred to it as "the kind of epistle one would expect from a clergyman of the most pronounced evangelicalism." Perhaps it was just as well that Severn received it almost two weeks after Keats's death.

[2] The third figure is blurred by the Italian date stamp: the postmark should be something like "F 107 21."

[3] To Haslam, January 15 (*KC* I, 197), Severn quoted Keats's lament, "this last cheap comfort—which every rogue and fool have—is deny'd me in my last moments."

→⫸ 43 ⫷←

J. A. HESSEY TO JOSEPH SEVERN
2 7 February 1 8 2 1

Address: Joseph Severn Esq/ Post Office/ Rome
Postmarks: F 21 154; CHAMBERY; ANGLETERRE; 19 MARZO

London Feb. 27. 1821

My dear Sir

I have undertaken to reply to your Letter of the 25th ult⁰ which you addressed to Mr Taylor [1] as I wish to spare him the uneasiness which he feels, and the depression of spirits which he suffers, whenever he hears or speaks of poor Keats. He is himself in much alarm respecting his own health, some very unfavourable symptoms having shown themselves in him. He desires me however to thank you for writing to him, and he hopes you will continue to do so. He wrote to you about a fortnight ago [2] to inform you that you might draw upon us in the usual way for One hundred Pounds on Keats' Account, as you will have so many heavy expenses to meet—This intelligence I hope has reached you, and has put your Mind at rest on that score—We saw your letter to Haslam,[3] and were much concerned that you should have suffered such distress of mind, even for a day, but as we had received advices from Dr Clarke [4] of a date prior to that of your letter, informing us that he had done all that was needful at Torlonia's we knew that you would soon be relieved from your Anxiety—The only fear we had was lest Keats should know of your distress, and we cannot say how much we both are gratified that it has been kept from him. He is infinitely indebted to you for all your kindness to him. I hope he is still alive, and still sensible of it—Your going out to Italy with him was I doubt not a merciful appointment of Providence for his benefit—you have been the means of keeping him alive, and I hope the term which you have added to his life has been blessed to his eternal benefit. I have always, even when I have heard poor Keats utter the most extraordinary and revolting opinions, had hopes of him—I always trusted that he would think & feel differently, and I cannot but still encourage the hope that you may have witnessed the change in his Sentiments, and seen its happy effect on his feelings— If it be so, how thankfully will he have acknowledged your kindness in saving him from the Effects of his Delirium—how will he have valued the little of Life you have given him—and how thankful will you have cause to feel that you have so rescued him. I hope my last letter [5] has reached you without any delay, and I much regret it was not written sooner, for though I should place but little confidence in the effect of any thing that I could say, yet a word of *truth,* however humbly expressed, may prove a word of Comfort to him that needs it.— Our poor friend needed it—O that it may have comforted him.— I can scarcely hope what I am now writing will reach you before our poor friend has quitted his earthly scene of trouble—Comparing the date of your letter with Dr Clarkes opinion of the probable duration of his Life I can scarcely suppose him alive even now—But if he should be still on this side of Eternity, O employ the time that remains in the only way that can benefit him—pray with him—pray by him—pray for him—and may the God of all grace & mercy hear your prayers & mine, and grant him pardon & peace through Jesus Christ. Do not start at these expressions—they come from my heart and are dictated by the earnest & anxious desire I feel for him—not for his life, for that is past hope—but for his happiness in that state of being which will never end. I write from my own entire conviction that nothing but Religion will bring a man Peace at the last & I trust you will bear with {me} when I venture to recommend my conviction to your {own se}rious Consideration also—I am very {very} sorry to hear of your own health having suffered from {your} attention to poor Keats—it is what we have long feared and we have been very anxious about it—Everyone here feels the most intense anxiety and Interest in poor Keats, and every one who knows and values him feels deeply indebted to you for your Care of him—Your next duty is now to take care of yourself—after such a period of labour & watching you will want Refreshment & Repose—do not exert yourself too much at first, or you will seriously injure your health—and when you are sufficiently recovered to pursue your Studies I hope you will derive all the benefit you could wish for from your residence in Rome—Pray let us hear from you soon—If our dear friend is still alive assure him of our most sincere and affectionate regard—Your friend Haslam is very well & so, I believe, are all your friends at Hampstead—Farewell my dear Sir—Accept my best wishes, and those of my friend Mr Taylor, & believe me, very sincerely Yours

J. A. Hessey

¹ For this letter of January 25 and 26, see *KC* I, 202–205. ("F 21" in the post-mark of Hessey's letter, as in Nos. 41 and 42, means "February 1821.")

² The letter of February 6, above.

³ Of January 15 (*KC* I, 195–200).

⁴ Evidently Clark's letter of January 13 to one Gray (*KC* I, 193–195).

⁵ Of February 12, preceding.

INDEX OF NAMES AND TITLES

INDEX OF NAMES AND TITLES

The names of George and John Keats, Joseph Severn, Valentin and Fanny Llanos are not indexed, but the titles of works by the first four are included.

Abbey, Miss, 13, 15, 18, 28, 31
Abbey, Richard, 1–6, 11–16, 18–21, 23, 25–29, 31–34, 39, 41, 58n., 62, 64
Abbey, Mrs. Richard, 3f., 15, 18, 28, 31
Abbreviated names and titles, 10n.
Adami, Marie Wilkinson (Mrs. J. G. Adami), 3n., 4, 7n., 8, 10n., 18n., 35n., 43n., 72n., 85n., 86n., 101n., 104n., 106n.
Agnew, Joan: *see* Severn (Joan)
Allston, Washington, 106n.
Alphonso XII, king of Spain, 104n.
Ampthill, Lord: *see* Russell (Odo)
Athenaeum, 63n., 104n.

Baroja, Pío, 58n.
Bastoggi Company, 82n.
Bathurst, Benjamin, 81n., 97n.
Beaumont, Francis, 24
Bedford, Duke or Earl of: *see* Russell (John, William)
Beilby, Mr., 28
Bewick, William, 8
Birkenhead, Sheila Berry, Countess of, 8, 10n., 75n., 85n., 86n., 88n., 97n., 98n., 101n.
Blackwood's Edinburgh Magazine, 65
Blanco, Francisco, 88, 90
Bliss and White, 53n.
Bonaparte, Napoleon, 24
Bonham, E. W., 78
Bourke, Mr., 11
Brawne, Fanny (Mrs. Louis Lindon), 3, 6, 10, 20, 24f., 30f., 33, 46, 50, 101f., 103, 111; *Letters*, ed. Edgcumbe (*q.v.*), 3, 4n., 16n., 18n., 23n., 56n.
Brawne, Frances (Mrs. Samuel Brawne), 20, 24, 30, 50; her family, 2
Brawne, Margaret (Mme. da Cunha), 20, 31, 50, 52
Brawne, Samuel, Jr., 3, 50

Briggs, Charles, 6, 20, 22f., 26f., 51f.
British Archaeological Society, 88n., 94
Brockmann, Ernesto, 81
Brockmann, Isabel Llanos, Countess, 7f., 75n., 81, 84, 87, 89, 94
Brockmann, Leopold, Count, 7f., 74ff., 78–81, 83f., 87, 89, 93, 96, 100
Brockmann, Mme. (mother of Leopold), 77
Brockmann, Miss(es) (sister[s] of Leopold), 78, 81
Brooks, John, 15
Brown, Charles (Armitage), 2, 18n., 26, 28, 29n., 112n.
Bull, John, 6, 49f.
Bull, Rankin, and Leight, 50n.
Butler, Grace Louisa Staples, Marchioness of Ormonde, 36
Butler, James, fifth Marquess of Ormonde, 37n.
Byron, George Gordon, sixth Baron Byron, 65

Casa Laiglesia, Marquis de, Spanish minister to London, 101
Castle Stewart: *see* Stewart
Cervantes, Miguel de, 21
Charles II, king of England, 31
Cheney, Ednah Dow, 106n.
Clark, Dr. (Sir) James, 109, 111, 116f.
Clark, John (of Enfield), 22
Clarke, Sarah Freeman, 105
Collins and Hannay, 53n.
Correggio, 77
"Courier" (ship), 12
Cuthbertson, Mr., 57f., 63

Day, Fred Holland, 13n., 102n.
Dilke, Charles Wentworth, 2, 4ff., 10, 30–33, 35–39, 41, 46, 48, 53n., 54, 56n., 58–61, 62n., 63, 65n., 66, 70n., 71f., 102n.

Dilke, Sir Charles Wentworth, 1, 10, 101f.

Dilke, Maria Dover Walker (Mrs. C. W. Dilke), 3, 18n., 20, 35, 38, 52

Disraeli, Benjamin, first Earl of Beaconsfield, prime minister, 104n.

Don Estaban, 54f.

Drury, Mary Taylor (Mrs. Michael Drury), 111

Drury, Michael, 2, 45, 112n.

Edgcumbe, Fred, 4, 10n. *See also* Brawne (Fanny), *Letters*

Eldridge, Captain, 12

Endymion, 22

Estaban: see *Don*

Every Saturday, 36n.

Eyre, General Sir Vincent, 100, 106n.

Fergusson, Sir Charles Dalrymple, 85n.

Fernando (Ferdinand) VII, king of Spain, 54, 57

Flacchi, Horace, 91

Fletcher, John, 24

Foreign Office ("F.O."), 84, 89, 95

Forman, Harry Buxton ("*F.*"), 1, 10, 12, 13n., 14, 19, 22n., 23, 29, 31n., 53n., 101

Forman, Maurice Buxton, 10n., 53n.

Franz, Alexander R., 75, 88n., 90

Franz, Francesco R., 74–77, 79, 88n., 90

Freemason: see *Sandoval*

Frere, Sir Bartle, 106n.

Frere, Mary, 101n., 106n.

Frith, Mr., 28

Furneaux, Henry, 90n., 97

Gale, Frederick, 81n.

Gattie and Peirce, 40

Gladstone, William Ewart, 84, 86n., 92, 100

Goodacre, Robert, 37

Gordon and Forstall, 26, 28

Gray, Mr., 118n.

Green, H. G., 35n.

Griffin, Gerald, 35n.

Gwynn, Stephen, 102n.

Halperin, Samuel William, 92n., 97n.

Harper's, New York, 65n.

Hartford, Mr., 53n.

Harvard Keats Collection, 1, 10, 102n. *See also* Paradinas

Harvard Library Bulletin, 43n.

Haslam, William, 2, 18n., 26, 28, 109, 115n., 116, 118

Hessey, James Augustus, 2, 10, 25–28, 111n., 112–118

Hodgkinson, Abbey's partner, 28

Hood, Thomas, 35n., 66n.

Houghton, Arthur A., Jr., 1

Houghton, Lord: see Milnes

Hudson, Harry K., 102n.

Hume, Martin A. S., 58n.

"Hyperion," 65

"Influence of Tea upon the Ladies," 72

"Isabella and the Pot of Basil" (painting), 9, 98n., 100, 104

Jeffrey, Georgiana Wylie Keats: *see* Keats (Georgiana Wylie)

Jeffrey, John, 105

Jennings, Alice (Mrs. John Jennings), 4, 11, 24

Keats, Alice, 105

Keats Circle (ed. Rollins, *q.v.*), 2, 4n., 6n., 10n., 16n., *et passim*

Keats, Clarence, 58

Keats, Ella (Mrs. George Nicholas Peay), 105

Keats, Emma Frances: *see* Speed (Emma)

Keats, Georgiana Emily (Mrs. Alfred Gwathmey), 16n., 17, 21f., 30, 34f., 39, 43, 52, 56, 58

Keats, Georgiana Wylie (Mrs. George Keats; later Mrs. John Jeffrey), 5f., 15–18, 22, 24, 28n., 30, 33, 35, 39–46, 49, 51f., 54ff., 58, 62, 64f., 67, 69f., 103, 105, 111

Keats, Isabel, 6, 24, 28, 30, 35, 39, 58

"Keats, John" (portrait, medallion, bust), 9, 98n., 100, 101f., 104, 106

Keats, John (George's son), 43, 58

Keats Museum, Hampstead Public Library, 102n.

Keats, Rosalind, 6, 15, 17, 21f., 30, 34f., 58n.
Keats-Shelley House, Rome, 53n., 65n., 102n.
Keats-Shelley Journal, 1n.
Keats, Tom, 4, 11, 24, 30, 52, 64, 104
Kenrick, Mr. and Mrs., 78
Koch, Felix J., 36n.

Landseer, Thomas, 8n.
Letarouilly, Paul, 75n.
Letters of John Keats, 13n., 18n., 29n., 53n., 85n., 86n., 101, 103, 106n.
Lewis, Mr. and Mrs., 35n.
Lindon, Herbert Valentine, 102n.
Literary Chronicle, 31n.
Llanos children and grandchildren, 70, 77, 79, 84, 87, 94f., 98, 100, 103, 105f.
Llanos y Gutierrez, C., 52, 55f.
Llanos y Keats, Giovanni, i.e. Juan (*q.v.*)
Llanos y Keats, Irene Louisa, 41, 43, 46, 52, 65, 70f.
Llanos y Keats, Juan, 7, 77, 79, 81, 84, 89, 93f., 98, 100, 103
Llanos y Keats, Louis Mariano, 53, 65
Llanos y Keats, Luis, 8, 77, 84, 86ff., 90, 95–99; his wife, 98
Llanos y Keats, Rosa, 7f., 81, 84, 87, 89, 92, 94, 96, 99
Longmore, George, 35n.
Louisville *Commercial,* 36n.
Louisville *Courier-Journal,* 106n.
Lowell, James Russell, U.S. minister to Madrid, 105

Manning, L., 1, 6, 36f.
Marcian Acqueduct, 8, 83, 87, 89, 98
"Marriage of Cana," 8, 80, 82, 85n., 87, 89, 94, 99
Mary, Princess, of Cambridge, 81n.
Melga, Mme., 78
Melga, S., 79n.
Mercedes, Princess Maria de las, queen of Spain, 104n.
Milnes, Richard Monckton, first Baron Houghton, 53n., 84, 86f., 94f., 100
Moore, Thomas, 65n.
Murray, John, 79n., 88n., 90n.

Narrative of Don Juan Van Halen's Imprisonment, 56n.
New York *Sun,* 105
New York *World,* 106
Newton, Sir Charles Thomas, 85n.
Norton, Caroline E. S. (Mrs. George Chapple Norton), 80
Novella, Emma, 8, 92
Novello, Vincent, 92n.

"On Woman," 73
Ormonde, Marchioness and Marquess of: *see* Butler

Paget, Sir Augustus, 94, 99
Palmerston, Lord: *see* Temple
Paradinas y Brockmann, Ernesto, 1, 6, 92n., 102. *See also* Harvard Keats Collection
Parker, John Henry, 88n.
Parker, Mr., 28
Parrish, Stephen Maxfield, 13n.
Philodramatic Society, Rome, 96
Piatt, J. A., 36n.
Pigot and Company, 70n.
Pistocchi, Alessandro, 81n.
Pius IX, pope, 9, 89f., 92, 94
Pope, Alexander, 65
Pope, Willard Bissell, 1n.
Prime Minister: *see* Disraeli

Quixote, Don, 21

Reynolds and Simmons ("R. and S."), 5, 57f., 63f. *See also* Reynolds (J. H.)
Reynolds, Charlotte Cox (Mrs. George Reynolds), 52, 66
Reynolds, Eliza (Mrs. George Longmore), 35n.
Reynolds, George, 66
Reynolds, Jane (Mrs. Thomas Hood), 35n., 66n.
Reynolds, John Hamilton, 1f., 5f., 23n., 32, 39–41, 47f., 59–62, 65ff., 70ff., 111; his family, 33, 35, 66. *See also* Reynolds and Simmons
Reynolds, Mariane (Mrs. H. G. Green), 33, 52

Rice, James, Jr., 2, 5f., 32, 39–41, 47f., 58n., 65f., 71
Richardson, Joanna, 102n.
Richmond, George, 7
Robertson, Eric, 85n.
Rollins, Hyder Edward, 10n., 13n., 43n. See also *Keats Circle*
Rossi, Signore, 76
Ruskin, John, 9, 91
Russell, John, first Earl Russell, 86n.
Russell, John, ninth Duke of Bedford, 75n.
Russell, Odo William Leopold, Baron Ampthill of Ampthill, 8, 74, 79
Russell, William, eleventh Duke of Bedford, 98n.

Sandoval; Or, The Freemason, 38, 52, 54f.
Santa Anna, Antonio Lopez de, 56n.
Scott, Sir Walter, **22**
Severn, Ann Mary (Mrs. Charles T. Newton), 9, 85n., 100
Severn, Arthur: *see* Severn (J. A. P.)
Severn, Claudia Fitzroy (Mrs. Frederick Gale), 80f., 100
Severn, Eleanor (Mrs. Henry Furneaux), 82, 86–89, 95, 97, 100
Severn, Elizabeth Montgomerie (Mrs. Joseph Severn), 9, 79, 81n.
Severn, Joan Agnew (Mrs. J. Arthur P. Severn), 9, 91, 94, 98
Severn, Joseph Arthur Palliser, 9, 77, 79f., 84, 87, 89, 91, 94f., 98, 100
Severn, Mary Dalrymple Fergusson (Mrs. Walter Severn), 82
Severn, unnamed children and grandchildren, 81, 89f., 91, 94–97, 100
Severn, Walter, 80, 82, 93
Shakespeare, William, 24; *Hamlet*, 50n., 70n.
Sharp, William, 8, 10n., 85n., 86n., 100n., 112n., 115n.
Shea, Henry, 67
Shelley, Percy Bysshe, 30; *Adonais*, 84
Shepherd, Mr., 83
Simmons (Symons), Reynolds and, 5, 57f., 63f.
"Sleep and Poetry," 65

Smith, Daniel, George Keats's partner, 66ff.
South Atlantic Quarterly, 36n.
Spain, minister of, to London: *see* Casa
Speed, Emma Frances Keats (Mrs. Philip Speed), 1, 10, 17, 21f., 30, 35, 39, 43n., 58, 95n., 101n., 103–106
Speed, Fanny, 104, 106
Speed, Florence, 104, 106
Speed, John Gilmer, 95n., 106
Speed, Philip, 104, 106
Speed, Thomas, 103, 106
Stewart, Edward, third Earl of Castle Stewart, 81n.
Stewart, Emmeline Bathurst, Countess of Castle Stewart, 8, 80f., 82n., 83f., 96
Stirling, Anna M. W., 7n.
Symons, Arthur, 58n. See also Simmons

Tallant, James, 25–28
Taylor, John, 2, 10, 25–28, 46n., 109–111, 112n., 116, 118
Temple, Henry John, third Viscount Palmerston, 86n.
Times, The (London), 81
Torlonia, Prince Alessandro, 109, 111, 116
Tuckwell, Gertrude M., 102n.
Turner, Joseph M. W., 9, 91
Turner, Mr., 34, 38

United States minister to Spain: *see* Lowell

Valeriani, Dr. and Mrs., 96, 99
Valeriani, Margherita, 96
Van Halen, Juan, 55, 57
Victor Emmanuel II, king of Italy, 8, 83, 85n., 89f., 92
Vilar, J. I., 99

W., W., 40
Watson, Mr., 66n.
Welford, Charles, 104n.
Wellesley, Arthur, first Duke of Wellington, 24
Whitley, Alvin, 66n.

Whittingham, Charles, 29f.

Whitworth, Charles, first Earl Whitworth, 23

Wilkinson, Charles, 2, 6, 28

Williamson, George C., 102n.

Winter, Miss, 83

Wood, Shakespeare, 88n.

Wood, Warrington, 106

Woodhouse, Richard, 29n.

Wordsworth, Dorothy, 10

Wreford, Henry, 80f.

Wylie, Charles, 14f., 28n., 42, 62, 70

Wylie, Mrs. Charles, 53, 70

Wylie, George Keats, 53

Wylie, Henry, 16n., 24, 41, 43, 46, 70

Wylie, Mrs. James, 16n., 70